JESUS:

superstar or savior?

Edited by JEREMY HARRINGTON, O.F.M.

Nihil Obstat:
    Rev. Hilarion Kistner, O.F.M., S.T.D., S.S.L.
    Rev. John J. Jennings, S.T.D.

Imprimi Potest:
    Very Rev. Roger Huser, O.F.M.
    Provincial

Imprimatur:
    ☩Paul F. Leibold
    Archbishop of Cincinnati
    March 22, 1972

The *Nihil Obstat* and *Imprimatur* are a declaration that a book
or pamphlet is considered to be free from doctrinal or moral
error. It is not implied that those who have granted the *Nihil
Obstat* and *Imprimatur* agree with the contents, opinions, or
statements expressed.

Cover design and photo by Lawrence Zink
Intaglio illustrations by Mark Barensfeld

SBN 0-912228-06-7
© 1972 St. Anthony Messenger Press

$1 fr, Bv. Carl 12-19-78

72-188255

Contents

Introduction

Christians have long been accustomed to believing in an "unpopular" Lord, or at least a Lord largely ignored by the marketplace, Madison Avenue, and the world of entertainment. But Jesus is unpopular no more. He has exploded onto the contemporary scene in an apocalypse of sight and sound that bewilders those who have long awaited his Second Coming, but never thought it would be like this: Jesus plays on Broadway, Jesus songs on popular radio stations, even Jesus bikinis.

Having grown up at a time when the proclaimers of Jesus were the Churches, not pop culture and the wire services, most of us feel disquieted, or at least confused, by all the Jesus phenomena surrounding us. Should the modern Christian be enthusiastic that the masses have finally "gotten religion" or cynical about the transformation of Jesus into a superstar?

In "Superstar or Savior," Karen Katafiasz probes the many facets of this puzzling Jesus movement: Jesus freaks; Jesus watches; *Jesus Christ, Superstar* . . . Hard questions are raised about some of the current interest in Jesus (its lack of intellectual depth, its neutralizing of Jesus by making him just another pop hero). Yet the author also finds positive values in the Jesus movement. For one, it forces each of us to rethink and rearticulate an answer to Jesus' question in Matthew's Gospel: "Who do *you* say that I am?"

With the questions and concerns of the Jesus movement as a springboard, each chapter provides challenging material for raising the level of our "Jesus consciousness." Personal testimonies of a highly diverse selection of committed Christians are presented to provoke the reader to prayerful reflection on the presence of Jesus in his life.

One of the most refreshing insights to grow out of recent interest in Jesus is a new appreciation for his humanity. In "Jesus: A Man for Men," Leonard Foley, O.F.M., prods us to put aside many of our taken-for-granteds about Jesus' divinity so that we might see Jesus through the eyes of the people who met him *before* his resurrection.

Can today's newly-surfaced appreciation for the humanity of Jesus stand the test of biblical evidence? Scripture scholar Eugene Maly helps us to a new understanding of our belief that Jesus is true God as well as true man by grounding this belief in divinity in the early Christian community's proclamation that "Jesus is Lord!"

Just as the early Christians came to their faith-understanding of Jesus through a process of community reflection, believing in Jesus today, or in any age, is essentially a *social* activity demanding the community of the Church. Karen Hurley in posing the question "Will the Real Jesus People Please Stand Up?" explains that authentic Christianity demands not only a keen awareness of the meaning and message of Jesus, but also a belief in his Church.

In the final analysis, the real Jesus people are not those who merely call Jesus "Lord" or even those who belong to the community that celebrates his risen presence in the world today. As psychologist William James demonstrated in his classic work *The Varieties of Religious Experience,* the only test of the authenticity of religious belief is the effect is has on the way a person lives his life and relates to other people. Theologian Kenneth Eberhard in "The Kingdom Begun" presents the serious moral challenge that Jesus poses to each of us in the concrete circumstances of our everyday lives. Belief in Jesus demands that we change our hearts—that we begin to live on Jesus' terms.

The 70's is an exciting time to be searching for Jesus: scripture scholars and theologians have numerous insights to share; pop culture offers a barrage of fresh ways of thinking and talking about Jesus; and a Jesus freak waits on a downtown street corner to tell us "Jesus loves you."

We offer this book, then, as an aid to today's Christian in his quest for mature faith.

Chapter I

Superstar Or Savior: The Puzzle Of The Jesus Movement

Karen Katafiasz

Last Christmas you could have given someone you love a gift to put him "with Jesus every minute of the day," in the words of some Los Angeles public relations men. A "Jesus watch" that sold for $19.95 carried "Our Savior's likeness . . . complete with ever-revolving crimson heart," and came in the "race of your choice." The businessmen responsible for the Jesus watch, it is reported, got their inspiration from a rubber, squeaking Buddha doll. "Wouldn't it be great if this were a rubber, squeaking Jesus?" they thought, and went on to refine the idea to something less outrageous and probably more salable.

The watch suggests a startling contemporary answer to Jesus' own question in Matthew's Gospel, "Who do people say the Son of Man is?"

American merchandising in the 70's has accorded Jesus a place in pop culture alongside Mickey Mouse, Snow White and Spiro Agnew. Jesus has become a folk hero, a social phenomenon and a gimmick to sell timepieces.

As bizarre as it may at first seem, the watch finds a comfortable niche on store counters next to all the Jesus pendants, buttons and sweatshirts. A Jesus movement is overtaking the country, or so the media has been pounding out incessantly. The founders of the Jesus Watch Company simply were listening to the clamor and grabbed a place on the commercial bandwagon.

The "Jesus movement," of course, is a big umbrella of a term that covers many types of believers, practices, even artistic events.

At the core of the movement are the Jesus people or Jesus freaks, estimated at numbering over 100,000 in this country, and described by *Time* in its famous cover story as "a growing number of young Americans who have proclaimed an extraordinary religious revolution in [Jesus'] name. Their message: the Bible is true, miracles happen, God really did so love the world that he gave it his only begotten Son."

The makeup of the Jesus people is more heterogeneous than that definition may imply. Some are disillusioned flower children who discovered Jesus after their Haight-Asbury dreams of love and peace turned into the nightmare reality of drug addiction and violence. Others are typical looking middle-class kids who might have played with pot to escape boredom and then found that accepting

Jesus as their personal savior was a thrill that lasted. Some of the Jesus people hardly heard his name before they joined the movement; others have staunchly Catholic, Protestant and even Jewish backgrounds. Some live in Christian communes that number about 600 across the country and demand varying degrees of asceticism; some, particularly the "straighter" believers, belong to well-organized groups, like Campus Crusade for Christ, Youth for Christ and Young Life, which have been respectable for many years; and some go it alone at home, often confounding their parents with spontaneous Bible-quoting and evangelistic zeal. Some groups demand strict isolation from parents, spouses, friends if they are nonbelievers; most encourage action in a world that needs conversion.

For all their differences, however, the Jesus people are brought under one heading by certain common beliefs and approaches. Though some are more fundamentalist than others, they all accept the Bible. "Jesus is God" is a key phrase for most of them, and few ever elaborate on it, caring little for theological interpretations or points of doctrine. What matters to them all is their encounter with Jesus as a real person—yet somehow transcendent—who offers warmth, compassion, peace of mind and whose life is to be studied and imitated. A strong emotional fervor—reminding one of revivalism and Pentecostalism—runs through Jesus people; they respond to their savior with both body and spirit. Their prayer meetings provoke speaking in tongues, personal testimonies, hand-clapping songfests and Jesus cheers ("give me a J . . ."). They reject drug use and sexual promiscuity as obstacles to salvation through Jesus, who is their "one way"—a favorite slogan.

The Jesus people are the dedicated center of the Jesus movement. But on the edge, perhaps, is where most of the general public personally confronts the movement; on the edge where the sounds of religious and quasi-religious songs drift from every radio, phonograph, concert stage and even night club, and where musicals about Jesus are box-office hits; in what may be called the pop culture of the movement.

Some two years ago, Simon and Garfunkel sang of a "bridge over troubled waters" that offered the comfort old-time spirituals usually associated with Jesus. About the same time, the Beatles released "Let It Be," one of their last recordings together: "When I find myself in times of trouble, Mother Mary comes to me. . . ." Acid rock, with its heavy, pounding electric beat was dying; a gentle, reflective sound that valued feelings of the spirit found eager listeners and hit the record charts.

These trailblazers eventually gave way to songs that were even more blatantly religious: to name only several, George Harrison's "My Sweet Lord," with its melodic mix of hallelujahs and hare krishnas; a Judy Collins' recording of the traditional hymn, "Amazing Grace"; a bouncy new spiritual that invites you to "put your hand in the hand of the man who stilled the water"; a Ray Stevens' novelty called "Turn Your Radio On," a kind of respectful parody of revival music.

8

But all these songs are like many BB's spraying the public compared to the cannon blast ignited by two English songwriters. In 1970, composer Andrew Lloyd Webber and lyricist Tim Rice recorded their rock-opera version of the last seven days of Jesus. (Even before this recording, Webber and Rice produced a virtually ignored religious rock work called *Joseph and the Amazing Technicolor Dreamcoat.*)

Jesus the Superstar

As most everyone knows by now, *Jesus Christ, Superstar* is today's idiom set to today's music. The character of Jesus is very much a man, who knows fatigue, depression, uncertainty and fear. He remains essentially passive in the rock work, carried along by the cries of the crowd, Magdalene's words of comfort, Judas' growing antagonism and eventual betrayal, and by the will of his God of whom he demands, "Can you show me now that I would not be killed in vain?" Though at one point Judas admonishes Jesus to "cut out the dramatics," the songwriters themselves have shown no such restraint. The Jewish high priests come across as incredibly mean and surly (enough to worry contemporary Jewish leaders that there may be a touch of anti-Semitism in the way their characters have been made villains). Herod honky-tonks a mocking assault on Jesus, and Judas is fleshed out into a well-meaning apostle, puzzled and worried by all "this talk of God."

Survival, according to Judas, requires caution and practicality: "When this whole thing began, no talk of God then—we called you a man." He berates Jesus for starting "to believe the things they say of you," for believing "this talk of God is true." The opera concludes with the crucifixion and an orchestral arrangement without words, titled simply "John 19:41." ("At the place where he had been crucified there was a garden, and in this garden a new tomb in which no one had yet been buried.") To the end, the divinity of Jesus remains a persistent question and, contrary to charges that Jesus is portrayed as *only* a man, the opera is ambiguous, making no statement either way.

Superstar's contemporary treatment of Jesus has incited controversy from the start, but at the same time it has gained monumental success. Over three million copies of the album have been sold. Several national touring companies have performed the music in concert to SRO audiences. Countless church and school groups, usually ignoring the copyright (to the composers' vexation), have freely used the songs. And a lavish (or, depending on the critic you read, vulgar, tasteless, irrelevant to the subject matter) Broadway production has been fashioned from the work by Tom O'Horgan, the director of *Hair* and *Lenny*. (Interestingly enough, the last, and maybe only other, stage show to grow out of an album was about another folk hero—*You're a Good Man, Charlie Brown*.)

With all its fictional padding and obvious dramatics, *Superstar* evidently offers something people want and are willing to pay for. It has even prompted another Jesus musical, called *Godspell* ("gospel" in Old English), loosely based on Matthew's Gospel. In *Godspell's* New York production, the performers wear clown makeup and Jesus appears in a Superman T-shirt. The staging has a carnival atmosphere, the songs are often lighthearted, and the effect is one of vitality and jubilation.

Unquestionably, in its commercial aspects the Jesus movement has triumphed. And its committed members are seeking new converts daily. But what do all the songs and watches and young evangelists mean to the person who believed Jesus was significant even before he hit the mass marketplace? Should Christians cheer that people who never owned a holy card or Sacred Heart key chain now see Jesus' picture in department stores and on their children? That many of the young have "gotten religion"?

Billy Graham, for one, welcomes the Jesus movement. If it is a fad among young people, he says, it's a "better fad than burning buildings." Norman Vincent Peale thinks the movement offers positive qualities—joy, exuberance, warmth, love. Prognosticator Jeane Dixon is "all for the Jesus movement," and predicts that young Jesus freaks "eventually will go back to the Church where they started."

But many feel puzzled. Comments on the movement from a recent *St. Anthony Messenger* readers' survey frequently showed ambivalence. "The Jesus movement seems to be a step in the right direction," went a common response, "but I'm not sure that these Jesus freaks have the correct concept of Jesus." A large majority of respondents over 20 years old admitted that something about the Jesus people's beliefs and life-style bothered them. And while most said they would *permit* a teenage son or daughter to attend a meeting of the Jesus people, they would not *encourage* them to go.

This kind of uncertainty is understandable. Some years ago, John Lennon, the most outspoken of the Beatles, tossed off a remark that the singing group was more popular than Jesus. Critics blasted him for glib irreverence, but he probably was speaking the truth. Ironically, today, when the Beatles no longer exist, Jesus is characterized as a superstar. And somehow it doesn't quite seem right: many Christians undoubtedly feel that Jesus was never meant to be popular in this way, as a kind of celebrity for the masses. And who would have expected it to have happened in an age termed the post-Christian era, riddled with cynical doubt and agnosticism, and among the generation that has denounced traditional, establishment beliefs and explored too many drugs and too much sex.

In a way, the ambivalence many people feel is a healthy reaction. There are both good and bad things to say about the Jesus movement, and a responsible evaluation—from the perspective of a Catholic in the 1970's—should maintain a balance.

The worst fallacy would be to dismiss the movement outright as religiously irrelevant because it is a part of popular culture. One respondent to the *St. Anthony Messenger* survey took this route wholeheartedly: "I do not see any relation between Jesus and pop culture. . . . The teachings of Jesus Christ, his doctrines and what the Catholic Church teaches will remain unchanged and firm. Pop culture is nothing but fads which will pass."

There are two problems with this line of thought: it rejects the idea that change and development in religious or spiritual matters is necessary and good; and it ignores the possibility that some passing cultural phenomena, whether fads or popular art, can be a source of real insight and encounter with God. The basis of Christianity may remain constant, but each age sees the Christian message from the particular perspective of its time, as well as in the context of tradition. The Good News of Jesus, in fact, can take on new shades of meaning for a man everytime he meets a new person or undergoes a new experience.

Much of the enthusiasm of Jesus people comes from their encounter with Jesus as a person, a fellow human. They cry "Jesus is my brother!" with the joy of suddenly discovering something wonderful they had never before considered. Similarly, one of the delights of both *Jesus Christ, Superstar* and *Godspell* is their very human portrayals of Jesus. For audiences used to the ethereal, waxy Christs of Hollywood, as in *The Greatest Story Ever Told* and *King of Kings,* experiencing Jesus in popular art as a man can be jarring and even religiously significant. Perhaps only once before did a popular art form do this very thing—Pier

13

Pasolini's film, *The Gospel According to St. Matthew*—and that received only limited exposure.

New York Times critic Walter Kerr caught the essence of this neglected approach in his review of *Godspell:* "After all these years of hearing and rehearing, of exegesis and apologia and conceptualization, we need some sense of a man . . . who moved, who put his feet against the earth with a push, who knew wheat as wheat and not as a noun in a parable, who took pleasure in the tangible, the muscular, the rhythmic, even in the giddy."

The Jesus movement just may be giving Christians a fresh sense of the man Jesus and of his life. It may, in fact, send them back to Scripture, as it did for two cast members of a *Superstar* touring company. The young people who sang the roles of Judas and Mary Magdalene disclosed in a local TV interview that after starting rehearsals for the opera, they read the Gospels with a new satisfaction.

Discovering Mystery and Peace

In a broader sense, the commitment of today's Jesus freaks reveals another need of our time fulfilled. In *The Making of a Counter Culture*, written in 1969, Theodore Roszak talked about a "youthful renaissance of mystical-religious interest." The young, Roszak said, are seeking the mystery and magical ritual that have been eschewed in our secularized technocracy. Some young people turned to drugs as a substitute for spiritual feelings. Many more became interested in the occult and mysticism, Eastern religions and yoga. The Jesus movement might very well be seen as the latest expression of this search. For Jesus people, there *is* a reality beyond this world and an existence beyond this life, and the Gospels are the source of their belief.

For many young people in the Jesus movement, the discovery of mystery in the person of Jesus has been incredibly "good news." The reports of confirmed addicts who painlessly abandon drugs in favor of Jesus seem endless. One parent answering the *St. Anthony Messenger* poll wrote movingly that a group of Jesus people changed her daughter's life. The girl had gone from weekend drinking, to drugs, to aimless drifting. Now, the woman wrote, her daughter "reads the Bible, attends Jesus meetings and feels that life is worth living again. . . . We are so very happy for her."

On a less dramatic, but equally vital, level Jesus people are finding an inner peace they never knew. "Jesus teaches me how to live my life," explained several Jesus freaks in the survey. If anything, their life-styles are a sign of harmony and naturalness. In a cluttered, hectic world, they have chosen what they believe to be important, what is good and true and most human. And their decision has released within them much visible joy, warmth and love. They seem to be living (to borrow a phrase from writer Eugene Geissler) as "part of the rhythm of the universe," and that's an admirable achievement for anyone in our time.

But as was suggested earlier, there *are* flaws in the Jesus movement, and they might all be summed up in the charge of superficiality. With all the emotional fervor, there is an undeniable lack of intellectual depth. It exists on the edges of the movement, where religion teachers happily play *Superstar* albums in their classes without offering any worthwhile evaluation and where groovy Jesus buttons quickly replace peace signs on denim lapels. Making Jesus the newest object of a personality cult neutralizes him. When his poster joins Janis Joplin and Frank Zappa on bedroom walls, he becomes mere entertainment and decoration; the challenge of his message is forgotten.

The absence of intellectual questioning is particularly obvious at the heart of the movement, among the Jesus freaks themselves. And they admit to the fact with a kind of pride at having chosen the "better" way. They exalt their own simplistic approach. One Jesus paper out of Cincinnati (there are about 50 such newspapers across the country) declares: "Theologians interpret the concepts of God and yet man goes to sleep still wondering why."

Theological concerns are not theirs; they insist on going, as Billy Graham says, "straight to Jesus" by reading the Gospels. Baptist minister Arthur Blessit, a gregarious leader in the movement, claims the Jesus people don't want a "watered-down Jesus" but the Jesus of the Bible: "born of a virgin, sinless, coming again." A fine concept, but unfortunately their fundamentalism often reaches the point of scriptural naïveté. The complexities of biblical study hold no interest for them. A Jesus paper surprisingly abounds with a lot of old, pious clichés that any self-respecting homilist would shun as ineffective and shallow.

Psychologist Eugene Kennedy has gone so far as to call their commitment "hysteria, not religion" because, he says, for all their emotion they show no profound faith or deep religious concerns. Other critics have accused them of copping out into an emotional, mystical unreality, "turning on" with Jesus instead of with drugs. In almost a childish way, many people want the person of Jesus to be vaguely awesome and thrillingly transcendent, as if he were some dark, occult power. (This willing mysticism has apparently penetrated cast members of *Superstar,* who seem quick to cite "divine" winds blowing during outdoor performances or being miraculously spared in a car accident.) They proclaim his divinity steadfastly. Some individuals in the movement have zealously scored *Superstar* and even the new rock spirituals for not forthrightly stating that Jesus is God. Yet few go deeper into what it means to say that Jesus is the Son of God.

Even fewer show any interest in Jesus as founder of a Church. There are some Jesus people who continue to belong to the denomination in which they were reared, but many tend to dismiss all institutional Churches as legalistic, complicated, overly concerned with money and competitive with each other. And such qualities, they charge, are only hindrances to encountering Jesus. Admittedly the Church has too often let the crustiness of institutionalism obstruct the fact that it is the living, believing community of Jesus. As a result religion has frequently taken on the appearance of being Church-centered rather than Jesus-centered. But in totally rejecting the Church, Jesus people isolate themselves into the present and their own limited religious experience, severed from history. They search out the biblical Jesus, only to forget that Scripture arose out of his community of believers.

In one of his columns, theologian Gregory Baum pointed out the serious difficulties of this approach: "What is typically Christian and Catholic," he wrote, "is that Jesus Christ rose from the dead, that he entered a new way of being, a way that permitted him to be present in the entire Christian community. Catholics believe that Jesus has, in his glorification, identified himself with the people of God. They are his body. He forms a single person with them. . . . The Lord is never separable from his people. That's why we say that we find Christ in the Church. The community of the brethren mediates the Lord to us." The Jesus people's rigid independence from the institutional Church focuses on some real problems of the Church. But, in the end, their extreme position appears as merely an irrational, gut-reaction, not deeply thought out.

The lack of intellectual depth within the Jesus movement seriously impairs its significance and endangers its future. All that emotional feeling may just become a little boring after awhile if it is intellectually hollow. And some Jesus people may easily shift their commitments to a different, temporarily more exciting leader-symbol. The adult religion that Christianity is demands profound involvement of the total person, and that necessarily includes a questioning mind, wary of falling into easy self-satisfaction.

The Joyous Search

"We are always becoming Christians," said Kierkegaard. The search for Jesus is an ongoing challenge for us all. It can't be wrapped up in any one religious movement or one instance of personal commitment, but it is as multi-faceted and lasting as our lives. We must remain open to God's acting in our time, through our culture, in other people. Long-haired, free-spirited Jesus freaks may re-awaken in us the joy and enthusiasm that is part of the Good News. The creators of *Superstar,* two young agnostics, may prod us to see the human Jesus by using a popular and widely accessible art form (a no less legitimate approach than that of their artistic forerunners who painted Jesus in medieval dress or surrounded by rays of light).

There, of course, will always be drawbacks to encountering Jesus through elements in our popular culture. They often constitute, as Walter Kerr says, inadequate—though forgivable—responses of men to mystery. Frequently they can be the products of men putting Jesus into their own image, as that of political revolutionary or anti-establishment drop-out. If they have flaws, though, they are probably flaws of our time. And we can learn from that, too.

Most of all, we must seek Jesus in the context of his faith community. Historian Hugh Trevor-

Roper has written that the Church created and continues to create Christ. For Trevor-Roper this seemed to diminish the chances of finding the authentic Jesus. For a Christian the very opposite is true: The Spirit has moved through the community of believers in significant ways for nearly 2,000 years; the Church is the fundamental arena for encountering Jesus.

We began this chapter by considering Jesus' question in Matthew. There is a second part to that question that must also be answered: "Who do *you* say that I am?" As we listen to the *Superstar* theme, when we're stopped on the street by an evangelizing Jesus freak, while we're reading an ad for a Jesus watch, we can start formulating a response. Gerard Manley Hopkins once wrote, "Christ plays in ten thousand places." Searching for him can lead to joyous discoveries.

Questions for Discussion

1.   What are some of the Jesus images currently exploited by American merchandising? Why do you think that Jesus can sell watches and bikinis? Do these merchandising images tell us anything about the kind of religious hero that today's Americans are looking for?

2.   Despite the many differences, what are some of the traits shared by all types of contemporary Jesus people? What factors might account for the appearance of the Jesus movement at this particular point in our history?

3.   How do you react when you hear a Jesus song on the radio? What is the image of Jesus that comes through in various Jesus songs with which you are familiar? Is this compatible with your own personal belief in Jesus?

4.   What is it about the Jesus people that bothers many traditional church-goers?

5.   Why does the author feel that Catholics should not reject pop culture outright as of no religious significance?

6.   Why are many Christians skeptical about Jesus' new-found popularity? Why does the author say," . . . Many Christians undoubtedly feel that Jesus was never meant to be popular in this way, as a kind of celebrity for the masses"? What does the author mean when she says: "Making Jesus the object of a personality cult neutralizes him"?

7.   What are some of the positive aspects the author sees in the Jesus movement? What are some of its flaws?

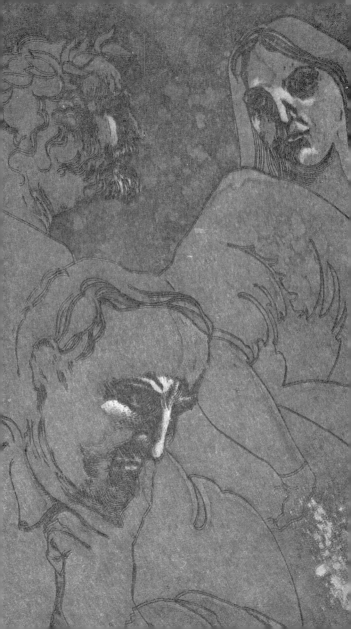

Chapter II

Will The Real Jesus People Please Stand Up?

Karen Hurley

Word association games can be very revealing. Often used by psychologists to probe the depths of the unconscious, this same technique can provide a handy tool for discovering the taken-for-granted associations that we make in our day-by-day living.

Several years ago a group of Catholic high school students constructed a word association test for their families and friends. Their secret purpose was to uncover the prevailing images about the Church today. The word *Church* was included in a list of 10 ordinary words, and participants were asked to say the first thing that came to mind when each word was read aloud.

Over 75 per cent of the respondents in all age groups associated the word *building* with the word

Church. Other frequent answers included "priest" and "Mass." Not one of the 750 Catholics polled answered "Jesus."

The irony in this lack of association between the ideas of Church and Jesus has struck me only in retrospect. The main concern of the students three years ago was the failure of Catholics to associate more person-centered images with the Church. They were dismayed that the post-Vatican II emphasis on the Church as the "people of God" had not made more significant inroads into everyday consciousness. Jesus wasn't an association that the class (or I the teacher) was even expecting or hoping for.

I wonder now why Jesus didn't fare better on those word association tests. After all, the relation between Jesus and the Church is fundamental. And yet today the term "Jesus people," which would seem to be a perfect word association for *Church,* sounds foreign to the ears of born and raised Catholics.

It is strange that a group on the very fringes of traditional Christianity, such as the Jesus people, can be distinctively identified by the name "Jesus." In some way this seems to imply that people within the organized Churches have not been conscious enough about defining their own lives in *Jesus'* terms, responding to *Jesus'* message, becoming aware of the presence of *Jesus* in their midst as risen Lord.

An important challenge presented to us Church members by the contemporary Jesus movement is to rethink our own relationship to Jesus: How does he affect our life here and now? How willing are we to have our identity as individuals and as a community tied up with his name?

Just what would we do if the question were put: Will the real Jesus people please stand up?

"People of God" or "Jesus People"

Because of Vatican II the predominating image of the Church has shifted from "body of Christ" to "people of God." This new key to the Church's self-understanding has brought a healthy change in consciousness. We now think of the Church more as a community and less as a hierarchical structure. But one very important thing may have been sacrificed with this shift in image. The Church as the "people of God" is in no way *explicitly* related to Jesus.

To be sure, we are the people of *God*. But this does not define us specifically as *Christians*. Other people are also *God's* people—the Jews being a good example. Today many theologians are beginning to speak about the unique relationship that God has with *every* community of people as it works out its own salvation history.

What then is distinctive about the way in which Christians are the people of God? We are the people of God who stand in a conscious relation to Jesus: Jesus is our Lord.

It is in terms of Jesus that we define our relationship to God: Jesus' Father is our Father; and we believe that Jesus is the final and perfect Word the Father speaks to us. It is in terms of Jesus that we understand the meaning of life: it is only through dying with Jesus that we live; Jesus is our hope. We are a community of people bound together by our common desire to live our lives in the mystery of Jesus.

Jesus is our reason for being together as a community, as a Church. The Greek word for Church, *ekklesia,* means a people called together. We are the people called together by God *in Jesus' name.* As the catechism puts it: Jesus is our founder.

It is in terms of Jesus that we are called together, and it is in terms of Jesus that we live together in community: it is his Spirit that makes us all one. The Church *is* Jesus Christ today. As St. Paul puts it, Jesus is the head, we are the body.

Obviously not all men stand in this same kind of explicit relationship to Jesus. Many people may know something about Jesus but do not believe in him as saving Lord; and many men have never heard his name.

Several years ago the German theologian Karl Rahner coined the term "anonymous Christian." He used this to describe the person who lives a graced life even though he has no awareness of Jesus, or at least does not consciously relate the meaning of his life to Jesus. Rahner pointed out it is not necessary that a person formally be a Christian to be saved. Any man who lays down his life in loving service, who responds to the call of the Transcendent in his life, is living his life on Jesus' terms—anonymously. Whether or not he knows Jesus or believes in Jesus, any man who discovers the fullness of life does so through Jesus.

In our present age of ecumenism we have emphasized the religious truths which all men of good will share, and we have discovered that there is much that we Christians have in common with Jews, Unitarians, Buddhists, Moslems, and so on. In this context it might seem unwise and inappropriate to be overly concerned about the lack of Jesus-consciousness on the part of Christians. Is it not enough that we are committed to love and peace, without explicitly relating these ideals to Jesus?

To point out that an explicit awareness of Jesus is not absolutely necessary for all men is not to say that it is unimportant for us. The Christian community has proclaimed Jesus as their message of Good News and as the norm for their common life ever since his resurrection because they were convinced that living life in *conscious* relation to Jesus made eminently good sense.

Love, peace, service to others, and so on, are all ideals that good men of every age and time have strived for. But how often have men made war in the name of peace or dehumanized other men in the process of serving them? We are human beings who need some concrete model to give our abstract ideals substance and direction. The life of Jesus the lover, the peacemaker, the servant, provides such concrete details.

Yet Jesus is not to be seen as an example for human behavior merely in the sense of a Gandhi or a Mohammed or a Martin Luther King, Jr. As St. Paul tells us, Jesus is the "first man" among men. He is the primary example of what it means to be a man because he is the Word made flesh, he is God-made-concrete in human life. Jesus challenges us to likewise make God concrete in our own lives and provides us with the original model for so doing.

Therefore Christians have a unique answer to questions about how to love, how to make peace, how to serve another: "Look to Jesus. He is the way, the truth and the life."

Before the resurrection when Jesus walked the roads of Palestine with his followers, they had together proclaimed the message of the Kingdom of God and its imminence: "Repent and change your hearts for the reign of God is at hand." Jesus used many parables and stories to concretize that message so the crowds would not miss the point, so it would not remain an abstraction having no impact on their lives.

With the resurrection new insight came to Jesus' followers: Jesus was risen; the Kingdom had come *in him;* the Kingdom was made concrete in him. Jesus *was* the very fullness of life that he and his followers had been proclaiming. Jesus' way of living *and dying* was the key to the Kingdom.

Therefore Jesus (originally the proclaimer of the Kingdom) himself becomes the new proclamation. The Good News the apostles preached on that first Pentecost—the earliest kerygma of the Church—was *Jesus;* Jesus is risen; Jesus is Lord; Jesus saves.

We are not a community built on abstractions. The very concrete, the very personal truth of Jesus' life is what gives shape to our own lives. The first fact of our existence as Christians is that we are a community based on Jesus. Without Jesus as our

defining reality we have no reason for being together as a community, as a Church. It is *in Jesus*
that we are saved.

On the one hand there is always the danger
that the Christian community will take Jesus for
granted, that his message will be lost in abstractions and "Church business," that he will be mini-
malized with an eye to ecumenism and the com-
monality of all religious belief. The contemporary
Jesus movement by focusing much attention on
the person of Jesus challenges us to avoid these
dangers.

But on the other hand there is the danger of
over-emphasizing Jesus to the point of negating
the centrality of the Church. Proclaiming Jesus is
not enough. Some Jesus people—both past and
present—have lost sight of the fact that it is only
within the community of faith, the Church, that
belief in Jesus is, in fact, possible.

Whether we choose as our guiding Christian
image that of "people of God" or "Jesus people,"
one point is equally emphasized: we are a *people*.
The covenant nature of our biblical faith demands
community emphasis, since a covenant is made
with a people, not with individuals. Perhaps this is
the challenge which traditional Christianity can
offer to believers in Jesus today.

Up with Jesus, Down with the Church?

A common question put to me by both high
school and college students as well as members of
the older generation disillusioned with the Church
goes like this: "I can understand why someone

would want to believe in Jesus and live as he did, but what does the Church have to do with it? In fact, doesn't the Church just get in the way?"

My answer: "Belonging to the Church is the only way I know to believe in Jesus."

The Church is important to me because I am an *historical* being. I stand at my point in history 2,000 years after Jesus walked the earth. The Church provides the needed historical link between the earthly Jesus and my life; and it provides the sacramental link between the risen Jesus and his action in my life today.

The Church is also important to me because I am a *social* being. I come to my personal knowledge and feelings about Jesus in large part because of the people around me—my family, my friends, my neighbors—and the Christian heritage which they pass on to me. Thus it is not just my contemporaries but also the men and women who have gone before me in faith that help to shape my attitudes toward Jesus.

My understanding of Jesus and my belief in Jesus are intimately bound up with a community of people, living and dead. It is within this community of faith that I encounter the memory and meaning of Jesus alive in Scripture and tradition; it is within this community of love that I can personally encounter the risen Jesus in liturgy and sacrament.

Belief in Jesus rests upon a very fragile vision of the world, one easily knocked apart by secular sensibilities. (Common sense says that a man cannot rise from the dead.) Without the support of a community of faith a fragile vision easily crumbles.

Jesus is present to us today, and we can meet him in the concrete circumstances of our lives. But we need concrete words and images—products of a community's dynamic of faith—to come to a full, conscious awareness of his message and meaning. Discovering who Jesus really is and what he has to say to us today is essentially a *social* activity.

This community activity of keeping Jesus' meaning and message alive is an on-going process. We, like the first followers of Jesus, must constantly reflect and create and test new ways and better ways to bring ourselves and others to the real meaning of Jesus.

The full meaning of any person's life is only apparent in retrospect. Notre Dame theologian John Dunne compares a man's life to a long, drawn-out periodic sentence which is fully understandable only when the final punctuation mark is placed. In Jesus' case the punctuation mark which made things meaningful was the resurrection. Only after this exclamation point could Jesus' followers begin to understand his full significance as they looked back over his life, prayerfully remembering his words and deeds. Everything became much clearer in the light of their Easter experience.

Those early Christians, under the guidance of the Spirit, had to search out words and images capable of expressing their new insights into Jesus. They called him Lord, Son of God, Messiah, Redeemer, Savior, Word of God, the New Adam. Thus developed the first Christology—that effort to express theologically the experience of the risen

31

Jesus. The New Testament with its variety of Christologies is the product of the apostolic Church's reflective experience of the earthly Jesus and the exalted Lord.

This process of reflecting on the experience of Jesus did not stop with that early community of Christians. Each generation in the Church has accepted what previous generations have passed on about Jesus; but they have also raised new questions, explained his lordship in different ways. This process of remembering and reflecting and rearticulating is essentially a *social* activity. It is the proper activity of the Christian community as a *people,* as "Jesus people." According to theologian John McIntyre, "Christology happens only within a believing community."

Christian understanding about Jesus arises out of the experience of Jesus in *community.* Within our Catholic tradition there has always been a certain thrust against overly privatized meaning. Thus our insistence on the teaching authority of the Church.

This tendency in the Church has sometimes backfired. Overinsistence on conformity in belief made a Spanish Inquisition possible. Overconcern with public meanings has sometimes meant that individuals failed to privately consider what Jesus meant and demanded in terms of their own lives. But on the whole, the main impetus behind this traditional emphasis is a healthy one: *my* understanding of Jesus is never the definitive one. Personal beliefs in Jesus must always be *tested* against the faith of the community—both past and present—and ultimately against the reality of Jesus himself.

Relevancy is one of the great values today. Many efforts are made to make Jesus *relevant* to our time and our thought patterns and our life-style. But there are limits to the ways in which Jesus can be cast to suit contemporary or personal fad. We can only go so far in making Jesus relevant to us; then *we* must change. We must make ourselves relevant to his message, to his thought patterns and to the life-style that his message demands.

Each of us has an image of Jesus and a personal understanding of who he is and what he expects of us. It is only through community sharing and testing that we can measure our own personal notions of Jesus against his reality.

We are not the measure of Jesus; Jesus is the measure of us. This is what the Church must constantly remind us.

Testing Our Jesus Images

It is particularly important to understand this community dimension of believing in Jesus in light of the current Jesus movement, where images of Jesus are developed and affirmed without reference to the wider community of Christian faith and Christian tradition.

Of course Jesus' meaning is inexhaustible. He can be all things to all men in the sense that he can offer every man the saving insight, the saving grace that is necessary to do the Father's will.

But Jesus is *real*. Like every real person, he has

33

a definite personality, he said certain things, his life had a particular shape in time and place. Thus to speak of Jesus as a political revolutionary is to distort Jesus; to say that Jesus was a preacher of "pie in the sky when you die" is to distort Jesus.

In our own time we have many diverse and sometimes conflicting images of Jesus—social activist, political revolutionary, guru, law-and-order man, "sweet Jesus." It is only the living faith of the community that can sort out the images. The Church "canonizes" what it recognizes as possessing real insight into Jesus; it declares as heretical what it recognizes as dangerous to a truthful insight into his meaning and message. It is only this community dynamic that can keep our understanding of Jesus based on reality rather than individual fancy or neurosis.

Such testing is a constantly occurring phenomenon in the life of the Christian community. It is illustrated in early times by the determination of the canon of Scripture.

We are all familiar with the canonical Gospels of Matthew, Mark, Luke and John. But these were not the only gospels written by early Christians. Other gospels, such as the gospel of Thomas, were rejected by the community because it did not adequately reflect their shared vision of the meaning and message of Jesus. While these noncanonical writings continued to be used privately, they never became the guiding force in liturgy and Christian education because they lacked community endorsement, that is, canonization.

We see this same testing phenomenon going on

throughout the centuries. Dogmas about Jesus were defined and certain understandings of Jesus labeled as heretical when the community of the faithful perceived a dangerous drift away from the reality of Jesus as they experienced him. Thus Jesus was dogmatically declared to be "true God and true man" in the fourth century to counter trends to de-emphasize or overemphasize one or the other aspects of Jesus' life and personality.

In our own day when a diversity of Jesus images —from superstar to law-and-order man—are arising, this testing activity of the Christian community must continue to take place.

A surprising result of a survey of *St. Anthony Messenger* readership was the importance that most people, even young people, attributed to the place of dogma in their religious belief. The question asked: Are the definitions (dogmas) of the Church concerning the relationship of Jesus in the Trinity and his human and divine natures important to you personally? Over 72 per cent of respondents over 30 years of age and 57 per cent of those under 30 said yes.

Of course dogmas are not the most important thing for believing in Jesus. But there is one important thing which might be correlated to a person's respect for dogma: his willingness to admit that there are certain limitations on what can be said about Jesus and that it is the community's faith, not private devotion, which speaks most authentically about the meaning of Jesus.

In the midst of the present-day Jesus phenomenon, it is important for us all to raise the level of our Jesus-consciousness. But it is of utmost importance that we do our consciousness-raising in the midst of the community of faith, for this is where Jesus—in his message and meaning—is alive.

Jesus is truly alive today. He is really present in our midst. But his presence is a *mediated* one, that is, it can be encountered only through the intermediaries of sign and symbol. This is an important qualification and points out another reason why believing in Jesus necessitates community life.

The notion of mediated presence, of sacrament, has always been central within our tradition. The Church has always insisted that there is no hotline to Jesus. We meet him only through signs—human signs. We meet Jesus through (mediated by) others, through (mediated by) the community of faith.

Soren Kierkegaard once said that the stumbling block of Christianity is the humanity of Jesus. It would be so much easier to believe in Jesus if he were just God. But to believe in another *man,* to see our salvation depending on another man, is a hard thing for our pride-filled egos to accept.

But the stumbling block of Christianity only *begins* there. The next point of difficulty is believing in the Church. Believing in the humanity of Jesus also means that I must believe in other men (in the plural)—in their ability to be mediators of Jesus, to be signs and sacraments of Jesus' presence among men.

To believe in Jesus means accepting the fact

that I can't save myself; but believing in the Church means accepting the fact that it can never be just me and Jesus. To have other men—both living and dead—involved in *my* salvation history is a hard thing for some of us to accept.

To be Jesus people we must let go of our egocentric dreams that all that is needed is me—we must let *Jesus* save us. But we must also let go of our equally egotistical desire that it can somehow be just me and Jesus—we must let Jesus save us *in community*. Jesus and his Spirit live in community. If we want to live on Jesus' terms, we must also live in community, the community of his Church.

It is difficult to allow ourselves to be saved along with other men, because people can be very difficult to put up with—from Curia bureaucrats to Pentecostals, liberals to reactionaries, pushy ushers to mumbling lectors. But somehow this is what believing in Jesus demands. The true leap of faith involves the affirmation that within these dry bones of a very frail and very human Church, the Spirit of life can be found.

We meet Jesus today in the visible community of his Church—in its liturgy and its sacraments. His saving presence pushes and prods us; he troubles us with the radical demands of his message. He reconciles us to each other and to the Father through his healing love. He fills us with joy and hope because we know that through him all forms of death and darkness are overcome.

But knowing that Jesus is really present in our midst should not make us complacent. He is present now, *but* he is still to come. This is a very basic paradox of Christian life—already, but not yet. And so we must continue to await his coming, to look for him, to change our hearts, to create a future for his coming.

The focus of Eastern liturgies, more so than in the West, is on this future coming of Jesus. Their Eucharist emphasizes that this is the breaking of bread *until he comes.*

This future orientation is essential to the Christian community. It makes us aware of the provisional nature of our existence now, and it makes us more aware of the importance of our relationship to our past, to our tradition. It is only out of the past that we can create the future. We remember so that we can hope. We look back so that we can look forward. Just as the meaning of Jesus and our belief in him can never be separated from the community of faith, so the community of faith can never be separated from its future and its past.

Church tradition is basically a liberating force in our quest for Jesus, not a repressive one. Tradition gives us a perspective on our present forms of belief and keeps us from being prisoners of the present. Because of this perspective we are free to change, to move forward, to grow.

The resurgence of ethnic consciousness is an interesting phenomenon of our time. People are no longer ashamed of their origins—in fact, they glory in them. We no longer have to apologize for coming out of the American "melting pot" still looking somewhat different. We can applaud our unique perspective on life whether Irish or Polish, American Indian or black.

Hopefully members of the Church are at a similar point of being able to glory in their unique self-definition in Jesus' name as well as to accept their past instead of running away from it. As the black culture and black history advocates have made all too clear, a person can only come to self-understanding when he accepts his past and carves a future out of it.

We American Christians are first and foremost "Jesus people." Without Jesus as the very explicit center of our self-consciousness, we have no reason for being. Good works of all kinds can prosper outside the Church. Social action, health care, education: all of these can be accomplished as well—some better—when not attached officially to the Christian community.

Our only reason for being is to sustain that community of meaning and healing love made possible by the presence of Jesus in our midst.

It is time we Christian people claimed Jesus as our own.

Questions for Discussion

1. In what way does the author see the new image of the Church as the "people of God" as unfortunate? What is distinctive about the way in which Christians are the people of God?

2. What does it mean to "live life on Jesus' terms"?

3. What is meant by the term "anonymous Christian"? Why is an explicit awareness of Jesus important?

4. What does it mean to say that Jesus was transformed from the proclaimer of the Kingdom to the proclamation itself? Why do we say that our Christian faith is primarily in a *person* rather than in abstract formulas?

5. What is the challenge that contemporary Jesus people offer to the Church? What challenge can the Church offer the Jesus movement?

6. What does the author mean when she says: "Belonging to the Church is the only way I know to believe in Jesus"? What would you say to someone who believes in Jesus but feels that the Church just gets in the way of authentic religion?

7. Why is discovering who Jesus really is and what he has to say to us today essentially a *social activity?*

8.   What does the author mean when she says that there has always been a "certain thrust against overly privatized meaning" in the Church? In what sense is this healthy? In what sense can this be unhealthy?

9.   Why must personal belief in Jesus always be tested against the faith of the community? How does this testing process work itself out in the Christian community?

10. What does the author mean when she says that there is no "hotline" to Jesus? How do you experience Jesus' mediated presence in your own life?

11. Why is the humanity of Jesus considered a "stumbling block" to Christianity by Soren Kierkegaard? Likewise, why is it so difficult for many people to believe in the Church?

12. Why does the author say that an orientation to the future is essential to the nature of Christian community? What should be the Christian community's attitude toward its past?

Chapter III

Jesus: A Man For Men

Leonard Foley, O.F.M.

Today we see Jesus through 2,000 years of faith, and the vision is true: he is the Risen One, the eternal Son of God. But he was also the Jesus of history, a man among men, and not many men who looked at him then saw a superstar.

The purpose of this chapter is to go back to Jesus' earthly life to see him with the eyes of the people of his day. What kind of man did Peter and the others leave their nets to follow? What did the shrewd theologians see, the sinners, the little people? What kind of man was it that loved Martha and Mary and their brother Lazarus? Whom did Judas betray?

It is important that we know the Jesus of history, the man as he was before his great "hour" of Calvary and Easter. That "hour"—his passion, death, resurrection and ascension—was the climax of his life. But it was filled with the spirit of all that went before in his ordinary life. So also, the great "hour" of our lives—our death and resurrection—is determined by the ordinary life that goes before. It is this everyday human life we want to study in Jesus.

When men looked at Jesus they did not say to themselves, "This is God: I want to see how God acts." They saw a man who made them realize the dignity of their own humanity. They saw a man free enough to say what he believed and courageous enough to take the consequences; a man on fire with dedication, yet often frustrated; a man who sometimes went hungry and sometimes dined with the rich; a man who amazed crowds, yet lost his own followers. Some of his contemporaries said, "Never did anyone speak like this man." Others said, "We will die for you." And still others said, "If we do not kill this man, he will pervert the entire nation."

We need to look at this man Jesus, for he tells us that it is good to be a human being, and that we can reach the divine only by plumbing the depths of our humanity. He showed us how a good and joyful life can be lived in the world *as it is.* He lived a fully human life by being completely alert to his Father's call in the reality around him, by being open to the needs of the people around him, and by maintaining his loyalty to his Father and a devotion to his fellowmen even when they seemed to ignore or turn against him. In short, Jesus was a man, *no matter what.*

I. "A Man Like Us"

What does it mean to be human? It means having flesh and feeling and spirit, a taste for the truth and goodness of reality, and the freedom to welcome them wherever they are found and wherever they lead.

To be human is to be born into a community of other persons, to learn to love and to be loved, to be one's own person and yet to be at the service of others. It is to move, to grow, to come to richer understanding and deeper conviction; it is to suffer the "slings and arrows of outrageous fortune" and yet maintain the joy of striving. It is to admit the limitation as well as the challenge of the moment; it is to decide *now,* in darkness or in light.

Like all children, Jesus developed gradually in humanity. He learned to love from the experience of the love of Mary and Joseph for each other and for him. He learned what it is to have a friend, to receive a present, to be cheated, to be laughed at. He knew a growing feeling of self-worth, of trust, of obedience. He learned to pray, to work, to watch and listen and imitate.

By the age of 12 he was a teenager thrilled to be in his Father's house, drinking in the wisdom of the teachers, asking them the frank and idealistic questions of youth. He took in the world around him—the little world of his home, the world of his friends and countrymen, the Romans, the lawyers, the gossips, the beggars. He knew the satisfaction of a day's work in the carpentry shop, the sweetness of Sabbath, the bitterness of having his

45

homeland occupied by foreigners. And he grew in the wisdom of men and the grace of his Father. His vision grew broader, his choices were firmer.

When we meet him as an adult standing among the penitents seeking the baptism of John, we find a man possessed with a vocation and a vision that has gradually matured over 30 years. He has a word for the world, a message about a Father's love and a Kingdom of peace. Had we been able to follow him during the ensuing months of his ministry, we would have come to know a man who was convinced that his words and actions played a central role in bringing the Kingdom of God to flesh-and-blood reality, and who came to see his mission as inevitably leading him to a death struggle with religious and civil authority. He moves courageously into a world where great faith and legalism clash, where both sin and goodness coexist, where crowds wait to be set on fire with hope one minute and clamor only for bread and circuses the next. He moves from day to day, from person to person, from experience to experience—and each person and event leaves a mark on him.

The fact of Jesus' moving and growing raises the question of his knowledge. How much did Jesus know? Did his divinity mean that his knowledge had no human limitations?

Here, for the moment, we are not looking at Jesus as the people of his day saw him. They knew him, first of all, as a man among men, and only after the resurrection did they come to a clear understanding of his divinity. The question of Jesus' knowledge can occur only to those who look back at the earthly Jesus already convinced that he is the Word made flesh, true God as well as true man.

The *St. Anthony Messenger* survey revealed that 59 per cent of the people over 30 years of age and 75 per cent of the people under 30 felt that Jesus had to reach maturity as we do by the process of gradual development. They were not disturbed by general statements pointing out that Jesus was ignorant of some things. But when the question was put more specifically, the results were quite different. Some 67 per cent of the over-30's and 57 per cent of the under-30's said they thought of Jesus as knowing all things even as a child, e.g., that he would die on the cross.

This paradox in responses points to a common difficulty. We know Jesus first through the categories of faith (Lord, Son of God) rather than through walking the roads of Galilee with him; therefore, we tend to understand his humanity in terms of his divinity rather than the other way around. Thus the question we raise is this: Did Jesus' mind work like the minds of all other human beings or did he have a built-in, given knowledge, especially of his divinity?

It is certainly inappropriate to assign encyclopedic knowledge to Jesus. Indeed, we cannot imagine the boy Jesus, while he is racing or fishing with the other children of Nazareth, carrying about in his head the tomes of Augustine and Thomas, the Code of Canon Law, all 14 volumes of the Britannica and the formula for the atomic bomb. The Gospels themselves do not think it

47

strange that Jesus should ask questions or grow in knowledge. They show him as having normal ignorance in ordinary matters.

No less a champion of orthodoxy than St. Cyril of Alexandria has said of him: "We have admired his goodness in that for the love of us he has not refused to descend to such a low position as to bear all that belongs to our nature, *included in which is ignorance.*"

But does this mean that Jesus did not know that he was the promised Messiah or the divine Son of God?

Father Raymond Brown, one of the most respected of American biblical scholars, points out that the normal human limitations on Jesus' consciousness and knowledge do not rule out his possession of some special insight into his divine sonship and his messiahship.

Jesus certainly was conscious of having a unique relationship to the Father and of playing a unique role in the establishment of the Reign of God. Father Brown holds that Jesus could have had this intuitive grasp of his divinity and his messiahship without this ever being clearly expressed in the forms of human words or images in his mind.

Thus it seems fair to say that Jesus was most truly a man in having to work his way through the details and concrete situations of his life just as we do, in having to make human judgments in darkness at times, no matter how *sure* his intuition of his unique relationship to the Father. As Karl Rahner points out, growth out of "not knowing" is one of the necessary factors of self-realization: "The fact of challenge, of going into the open, of confiding to the incalculable, [the fact] of the obscurity of origin and the veiled nature of the end—in short, of a certain kind of ignorance—are all necessary factors in the very nature of . . . self-realization."

We can understand this description of Jesus' knowledge in terms of our own lives. We too are *sure* of something—that the Father loves us in a special way, that we are his adopted sons and daughters, that we will rise again. But we, like Jesus, are still faced with the challenge of working out the details, of growing in wisdom and knowledge so that we can better understand the specifics of God's will for us.

Despite the certainty of our intuition and the strength of our trust, the step into the darkness of death is still a fearful one. And so it was for Jesus. We cannot imagine Jesus putting on an act in Gethsemane or merely quoting a psalm on the cross where he cries, "My God, my God, why have you forsaken me?"

To be human is to decide in freedom, to choose between alternatives. Jesus would not have been truly human if he had not had to make choices, either because he was being dragged through life as a puppet on a string or because he knew beforehand what was going to happen in every instance and so could "arrange" his life with perfect foreknowledge.

He had to decide in the half-light of uncertainty and ambiguity; he had to risk and to dare.

49

He had to make up his mind what *in particular* the Father's will was here and now. For example, when people wanted to make him king, he had to reflect whether this was the Father's will for him. He retreated to the mountains to pray and decided that political messiahship was not for him. He had to decide what to say to the restless crowds; he had to decide when it was prudent to remove himself from the public scene and when it was time to walk into mortal danger in Jerusalem.

Every day brought him almost infinite possibilities of misunderstanding, failure, betrayal, surprise and pain. He had to bide his time, wait, go from day to day.

So, returning to the viewpoint of the people of his day, we see Jesus as an extraordinary man, but one whose mind must seek and probe, consider alternatives and sometimes not know all the facts. He suffers doubt and perplexity, and even chooses a man named Judas. We see Jesus as a man on the march to fulfillment. He is the adult and mature man, always total in his commitment yet always enriched and deepened by each day's new experience. He is always a man going to his Father in love but taking one step at a time. In short, there is always a way in which he can be more fully possessed by his Father's love.

His is a life of movement in history, with process and progress toward fulfillment. He moves through his life to the place where the precise circumstances for his total and final giving are made evident. And he *chooses* to go to Calvary after the agonizing decisions of Gethsemane.

II. *"Tempted as We Are in All Things"*

Because Jesus had to choose just as we do, he knows how difficult it can be to make the faithful choice and how easy it can be to do our own will rather than the Father's.

The author of Hebrews says of Jesus: "Since he was himself tested through all he suffered, he is able to help those who are tempted" (Hebrews 2:18). How was Jesus tempted?

Jesus, like each of us, was tried by the power of evil. The Gospels relate very dramatically the scene of Jesus being tempted in the desert to use his favor with God for his own advantage rather than in the service of others. Like any man, he knew how pleasant it would be not to suffer the consequences of selfless service or the consequences of telling the truth. He was tempted like any good man by being made to know *how costly it is to be faithful.*

Because Jesus made a whole lifetime of faithful choices, he could do nothing but pay the price: powerlessness, poverty, loneliness, misunderstanding . . .

Totally involved in the human condition, Jesus felt the common pain of being misunderstood. He suffered as all men do, not only from malicious untruth but also from the distortions and prejudices which can become so much a part of a religious or civil culture that they are accepted as truth.

A large part of the Gospels show Jesus rejecting the persistent attempt to make him a political-religious messiah, the only kind most Jews could

51

contemplate. Even those who should have known better never seemed to catch on. At the very end, the apostles were still talking about swords and a Kingdom that was indeed of this world.

For all his insistence on service, Jesus saw his followers quarreling like children as to who was first among them. The mother of two apostles secretly tried to get her boys promoted to the Number One and Number Two positions in the Kingdom! The apostles tried to keep the "wrong" people away from him—children, the blind, a Gentile mother. They raised their eyebrows when they saw him talking with a Samaritan woman. He had to be patient with men who questioned why they could not cast out devils as he did, and with those who followed him with an eye on the bread of earth rather than of heaven.

He knew the rejection of his own home town, the people he had grown up with. He no longer talked their language. "He could work no miracle there, apart from curing a few who were sick . . . so much did their lack of faith distress him (Mark 6:5). At one time his own relatives thought he was out of his mind—with zeal, of course, but mad, nevertheless.

He knew the pain of being suspected, rejected, hated because he bore witness to the truth—and to the untruth of some men's lives. He saw himself gradually being caught in a web of futility, ignorance and deliberate misunderstanding. He knew the supreme insult of being accused of collusion with the very forces of evil he would destroy: "He has a devil and he is mad. He casts out devils by the prince of devils. . . . He seduces the crowd."

He wept over a Jerusalem that did not understand; he had compassion on the victims of ignorance and untruth, the people wandering through life without a purpose, like sheep without a shepherd.

Not even his friends understood when the crisis came—his "hour"—the ultimate confrontation to which his commitment led him. The aloneness suffered by every man weighed upon Jesus in his solitary, prayerful struggle in the garden of Gethsemane. He knew the sense of human "distance" from the Father. He was alone, with a vivid consciousness of man's condition: totally dependent on the Father, yet at the same time terrifyingly caught in the grasp of evil and doomed to the final slavery of death.

Where was it all leading? Had he taken the right road? What would happen in the dark night of death? Here is man deprived of all the pain-killers and material supports of life. But Jesus does not despair. He maintains his confidence in his Father's love, no matter what.

He shows his brothers and sisters the fundamental hope that every man can find at the bottom of despair. "Father, I cannot drink this chalice of pain and death. But, Father, you are on my side. You know . . . you know . . . I trust you."

After the peak experience of Gethsemane, Jesus must now go through the no-longer-dramatic process of paying the price of his courage and loyalty to the Father, and paying the price that love of his fellowman will demand. When the showdown

53

comes, his friends run away. Like millions before and after him, he knows what it is to be caught in the power of the club and the whip. He knows the terror of back-room beatings and degradation, the sneers of the righteous, the contempt of the powerful, the careful legality sending him to death, the "I'm helpless" shrug of a Roman politician.

He knows the fear that grips a man's heart when a mob yells for blood or a prison door clicks with finality. Jesus, an authentic man, is a victim of others' charades.

Flesh and spirit suffer agony together. He knows the pain of thorns and nails, the power of death slowly possessing his body, the muscles going helpless, breathing becoming impossible . . .

The cross has now become an honorable sign to Christians. When Jesus died, a cross had no dignity. It was the mark of total disgrace. Even his friends must have wondered a bit, how it could end so—crudely. *Was* he just a freak, a foolish visionary as demented in his own way as the rest of the riffraff who ended on crosses? The "all-American," the "almost-President," the promising young leader found dirty and dead. Maybe. . .

But he proved that there was no power but his Father's. When the power of evil was at its mightiest, he loved and he hoped. He had to plunge into the darkness of death just as each of his brothers and sisters would have to do. Yet he knew that the Father was there waiting. He trusted. But it was a trust that had to be given in the dark night of death.

Jesus was misunderstood, he was tempted, he

was lonely, he was afraid. He lived the whole of the human condition, including being tried by the forces of evil, so that he could heal it. He brought all men salvation by being *a faithful man,* no matter what. He stood with his brothers and sisters and, like them, was attacked and apparently destroyed by evil. But because he was completely receptive to the gift of life as his Father gave it, he broke the grip of suffering and death for himself and for all his brothers and sisters.

There would never be a man or woman who could not look up from misery and see hope: men in animal cages, Biafran mothers with babies starving at their breasts, a soldier dying on a senseless battlefield, a rich adulteress or a poor widow, a desperate king or a daughter who can't go home. They can all look at one who suffered their helplessness in the face of evil. And every one of them would be able to know the secret of being saved from it all: to let the healing love of a Father pour into their hearts from within. To trust, to hope, to love, no matter what.

III. *"I Have Given You an Example"*

Above we have seen Jesus under two aspects: as sharing our "normal" and our "suffering" life. How can we now describe the unique human spirit that filled his life? Can we pinpoint his consistent human attitude so that we can make it our own? Perhaps we can sum it up in four images: Jesus as a mature child of the Father, Jesus as free man, Jesus as Good Samaritan, and Jesus as the sign of the forgiving Father.

First of all, Jesus' life is summed up in his total love and devotion to the Father. This was the joy and consuming passion of his life. "My food is to do the will of him who sent me."

He kept the First Commandment. He loved his Father with his whole heart and soul and strength, in darkness and light, with childlike trust and immovable courage. And in this he showed us what it is to be a man: not just one possessed of body and spirit, but one who lets body and spirit freely be possessed by the love of the Father.

To be a man is to have a center of life, a kingdom and a Father to turn to in absolute trust. Jesus' "good news" was that we have a Father who knows our needs and fulfills them with infinitely more graciousness and faithfulness than he shows in the painting of flowers and the feeding of sparrows. Life is a gift. God's glory is a living man who appreciates and makes use of the gift.

Secondly, Jesus is a totally free man: that is, he is ready for the truth of every situation and open to the needs of other men. He is not enslaved by selfishness or outside pressure—social, political, economic or religious. He awaits the Father's direction on how to respond with love in each situation: an outcast crying for community, leaderless sheep needing a shepherd, an adulteress needing dignity, religious leaders needing a rebuke, 12 fainthearted men needing conviction.

Jesus is free enough to be seen at the table of rich Pharisees as well as in the noisy bars where "sinners" gathered. He is not threatened by the inquiring tricksters of law or by Samaritan prostitutes, by agonized souls seeking a meaning in life or sisters mourning a dead brother. He is at ease with Roman centurions, children, tax gatherers and the holiest mother who ever lived.

He is free enough to speak simply. He did not construct an esoteric system of philosophy to encase his teaching: it was himself, here and now, free and alive. He spoke a language that both housewives and laborers could understand, about wineskins and plowing, wheat and weeds, sheep and birds and flowers—yes, bellies and privies.

He is free enough to be angry. He could let himself speak out against hypocrisy and legalism. And he could express his frustration: "How long will I be with you?"

He was free enough to tell his followers plainly that he would suffer and die, and so would they. He did not water down his teaching in the face of mass desertions. When he judged that his hour had come, he walked into the midst of his enemies.

His freedom disappointed some. He needed no power base and avoided every hint of political involvement. The whole Gospel of Mark is characterized by the "Messianic secret," a deliberate discouraging of efforts to see Jesus as the traditional Messiah. When men came crowding to make him king, he hid in the mountains. "Tell no one" was the word to all whose limbs he straightened and whose eyes he opened.

He was free; he was courageous. He was simply devoted to his Father.

And freedom is costly; it demands endless searching and the daring to go into unexplored darkness. "Jesus did not live according to some divinely constructed plan spread out before his eyes, but by the will of his Father as he encountered it at every step he took in going to meet his 'hour.' What can happen in a human life that is determined by all this? The answer must be: anything and everything." Thus Romano Guardini sees the free Jesus.

"God's will" is all about him and within him, and no man or devil can stop him from embracing it.

A third characteristic of Jesus was his love for his fellowmen. To be a man like Jesus is to move freely in truth and love, to love like "the first-born of many brothers," to be a "good Samaritan."

Jesus was so possessed by the vision of his Father that he could do nothing but show that Father's tenderness and concern to all his brothers and sisters. That love is shown in two ways: caring for every need and healing every wound. It is concretized in a story that Jesus told: the parable of the Good Samaritan.

The Good Samaritan is the man who spends himself being concerned with the needs of others *as they come,* who never knows what lies around the next corner. He is simply ready to concern himself with whatever brother or sister happens to be present. Jesus is the Good Samaritan.

To be fully human is to imitate the love we see in Jesus.

A fourth aspect of Jesus is that he was the human sacrament of the Father's forgiving love. To be a man like Jesus is to act like the Father:

"His sun rises on the bad and the good, he rains on the just and the unjust." As a man totally devoted to his Father, Jesus fulfills the deepest desire of the Father: that his children be reconciled to him and believe in his mercy.

The story of the prodigal son provides us with a model for being as human as Jesus. Jesus is like the father who forgives his runaway son. Thus he expresses the great dignity of human beings: they can forgive like the Father.

Among men, to forgive may merely mean to refrain from revenge; with God, it can only mean continuing to love us as he always has. He does not have to decide to forgive us. His nature is to love, and in loving to heal.

Jesus simply said to Peter when he met him after the betrayal, "Do you love me?" That is the only condition for forgiveness—and it lies on man's side, not God's.

Jesus was fully a man because he forgave; he forgave because he was fully a man. He was open to the needs of others and the will of his Father to reconcile them. He forgave by being alert to the deepest reality, the hunger of men to be healed and alive.

At the end he summed it up: "Father, forgive them. Your forgiveness flows through me, because I am a man fully in your image."

Each of us is a man, a sign of life going in courage from our own Bethlehem to our own Calvary; a body alive to the real, though tasting it only one day at a time; a spirit powerful enough to love in joy and to move toward the light in spite of pain and wrong turns; a sacrament of the love and forgiveness of the Father.

Essentially two things are the test of a man: faithful, trusting love of the Father who made him, and unselfish, forgiving love of his fellowman.

Jesus summed it up in two prayers on the cross:

"Father, forgive them, for they know not what they do."

"Father, I put my life into your hands."

Questions for Discussion

1.   What does the author mean when he says that contemporary Christians see Jesus "through 2,000 years of faith"? How does this make our perspective on Jesus different from the perspective of those who knew Jesus before his death and resurrection?

2.   When the men of Jesus' day looked at him, they did not see a god, but a man. What kind of man did they see?

3.   Do you think that Christians, over the centuries, have lost sight of this human Jesus? Why?

4.   What does the author mean when he says that Jesus tells us "we can reach the divine only by plumbing the depths of our humanity"?

5.   Why is the question "How much did Jesus know?" only a concern for us and not a concern for those who walked the roads of Palestine with Jesus? Why is it hard for many people today to accept the fact that Jesus did not know all things?

6.   In what sense is the following statement cor-

rect: Jesus did not know he was the divine Son of God or the promised Messiah? In what sense is it incorrect?

7. According to Karl Rahner, growth out of "not-knowing" is one of the necessary factors of self-realization. How was this true in Jesus' life? (Give some examples of Jesus making decisions in the half-light of uncertainty and ambiguity.) How is this true in our own lives?

8. The author says that "Jesus made a whole life-time of faithful choices. . . ." What is a *faithful* choice? How was Jesus tempted to be unfaithful? How are our temptations similar to his?

9. Why was Jesus misunderstood by the people of his own day? Why will there always be the danger that we will misunderstand Jesus' meaning and message?

10. What does it mean to say that Jesus "knew the sense of human 'distance' from the Father"? Did Jesus have a clear knowledge of where the events of Gethsemani and Calvary were all leading him?

11. What was it about Jesus that was able to heal the human condition? In what sense does Jesus' life contain the secret for our own salvation?

12. The author chooses four images to pinpoint the consistent human attitudes of Jesus. What can we discern from each of these images to make a part of our own lives?

Chapter IV

Jesus Is Lord!

Eugene H. Maly

Who was Jesus of Nazareth? The question has been asked throughout the history of Christianity, but perhaps never with such passionate interest as today. And the answer being given with greater insistence than before is that he was a man, a mysterious and misunderstood man, perhaps, but still a man, with all the cares and concerns, the anxieties and hesitations, the doubts and temptations of every man.

Revolutionaries and social activists, humanitarians and cultural prophets all claim him as "their man," the model of their aims and their methods. He is the superstar in the great game of life, the reluctant hero in the struggle for human progress. The man Jesus stands center stage in the world drama and many are finding this the most fascinating experience in their religious lives.

To a generation brought up on a faith in Jesus as Son of God, the Second Person of the Blessed Trinity, true God as well as true man, this new insistence comes as a shock if not as outright blasphemy. Indeed, a recent survey of *St. Anthony Messenger* readers reveals that it is still the concept of Jesus as divine that is most easily accepted by people of all age groups.

Is this picture of a haunted, hunted, human savior in accord with the biblical evidence? One of the earliest formulations of Christian belief found in the New Testament was expressed by St. Paul in this way: "Even though there are so-called gods in the heavens and on the earth—there are, to be sure, many such 'gods' and 'lords'—for us there is one God, the Father, from whom all things come and for whom we live; and *one Lord Jesus Christ,* through whom everything was made and through whom we live" (I Corinthians 8:5-6; italics added). Christian history has shown that when this profession of faith in Jesus as Lord has been made with the same vigor and conviction as Paul's, Christianity has flourished. When it is questioned or watered down, Christianity is weak and floundering.

The results of the *St. Anthony Messenger* survey indicate that many today are fearful that Christians are not vigorous enough in their proclamation of Jesus' divinity. Seventy-four per cent of respondents over the age of 30 answered "yes" to the question, "Do you think the emphasis on Jesus' humanity is overshadowing His divinity?"

Concerns such as this have led theologians to

re-examine the evidence of the Scriptures and the early Church for the divinity of Jesus Christ. In the process they have recognized, perhaps more clearly than before, the reality of Jesus' humanity and at the same time the early Christians' conviction that this human Jesus is Lord. Is this the same as saying that Jesus is God, that he has a divine nature, that he is the Second Person of the Trinity?

There are two principal difficulties with this type of question. The first is that it presupposes a mentality that was foreign to the biblical writers. In other words, the earliest Christians would never have asked how many natures there were in Jesus Christ, or whether his person was human or divine.

It was only later, when philosophically-minded people began asking that kind of question and when some of the answers being given threatened to destroy the core of the Gospel message, that the Church had to formulate her own answers. For example, when certain writers spoke of a mixing or confusion of the divine and human natures in Christ, the Council of Chalcedon (451) clearly defined the doctrine of the two-fold nature. Even before this, Arius had denied that Jesus was truly God and had said there was only one nature in him. The Council of Nicaea (325) responded by a statement that we still recite on Sundays and other feast days at the Eucharist. But these and other Councils were responding, and rightly so, to particular questions asked at a particular time in history. They were only presenting in another form what was already contained, in some way, in the Scriptures.

The second of the principal difficulties in responding to this kind of question asked about Jesus is the difference in the theological concerns of the early and later Church. The theology of the New Testament is a preacher's theology; it is almost exclusively functional in its approach. In other words, it was not concerned with the inner life of the Trinity in itself but only insofar as the Father, Jesus, or the Spirit related to man. Even when John calls Jesus the *logos* or Word, a term that could be conceived to have deep philosophical meaning, we can see his concern as being to describe the Christ as one who comes forth from God and who is to be heard and responded to by man.

It was only later that a different theological concern began to manifest itself, a concern for precise definitions and formulations. We might, in contrast to what we have called the preacher's theology of the Scriptures, call this a philosopher's theology. This was when the Apostles' Creed and the Nicene Creed we say at Mass came into being under the guiding light of the Holy Spirit. This development was a legitimate and necessary one, occasioned by the distortions in doctrine that were already beginning to appear in the second half of the first Christian century. Without such definitions Christianity as a whole could have suffered the fate of some of its sects, which simply faded out of existence.

This doesn't mean that the Church now abandoned its preaching role to confine itself to formulating definitions. The New Testament concern to preach the Gospel to all men remained the basic concern of the Church. It was because of the real danger that the Gospel would be distorted that the Church had to engage in defining doctrine. These definitions are, of course, a later development, and because of this it is not possible to ask the same question of the creeds that we can ask of the Bible. Or better, the creeds and the Bible will not give the answer in the same way.

A Lordship of Creative Love

To understand the meaning and importance of our present day statements about the divinity of Jesus, we must first examine the meaning of the scriptural statement from which it developed, the statement "Jesus is Lord." The concept of lordship in the early Church is not an easy one to understand. But unless we come to grasp it in some way, we will never be able to appreciate the basic Christian profession of faith in its radical and far-reaching consequences.

To appreciate properly the New Testament doctrine of the lordship of Jesus Christ, we must see something of the Old Testament background. It was always in the context of that literature that the early Christians thought and wrote. And one theme stands out most clearly in that literature, namely, that God is Lord. The title of Lord, either in its original Hebrew form or in the interpretation of the name Yahweh, is found over 5,000 times applied to God. Basically, lordship meant complete ownership, and God was thought to be Lord of heaven and earth and all that is in them because he had made them and they belonged to him.

There is a uniqueness to God's lordship in the Old Testament. First, no other god could be called Lord in the same way as Yahweh. There were many reasons why Israel believed this, but it is evident in the fact that she attributed everything to his creative activity and in the fact that she called him "Lord of lords" (cf. Psalm 136:3). Second, God's lordship was exercised in a special way over his people, Israel. It is just because Yahweh is their Lord that Israel could be his "special possession, dearer to me than all other people, though all the earth is mine. You shall be to me a kingdom of priests, a holy nation" (Exodus 19:5-6).

This uniqueness of God's lordship is important. It is not a lordship whereby ownership means oppression or tyrannous domination. It is, rather, a lordship that creates something in the subject, as the text from Exodus, quoted above, indicates. Divine lordship, precisely because it is divine, brings the one possessed into a new dimension of being and of life. He is brought into the liberating sphere of the non-world, the divine.

The term that the Greek translators of the Old Testament used to express the lordship of Yahweh was *Kyrios*. The word was used in the Greek world to designate kings and other rulers. It was not, however, used of the Greek gods until some time later (in the first century B.C.), since their gods were not thought of, as the Hebrew God was, as personal creator or as having anything to do with the fate of man and the world. The biblical usage, therefore, suggests a unique sense in which God's lordship was understood.

When we come to the New Testament and find the word *Kyrios* used of Jesus in the same sense that it was used of Yahweh in the Old Testament, there are some important consequences. For one thing, it would be a valid conclusion to say that calling Jesus Lord is equivalent to calling him God. His divinity is implied in his lordship. Also, we can legitimately conclude that Jesus' lordship was not conceived of as one of oppression or restrictive domination, but rather as one of creative love, just as the Father's was in the Old Testament. The point of community, then, between Jesus and the Father is admirably expressed in their common lordship.

The clearest expression of the divinity of Christ appears to be the response of Thomas to Jesus after his ressurection: "My Lord and my God!" (John 20:28). Here lordship and divinity are combined. And again, this combination (*kyrios* and *theos,* "Lord" and "God") is found in the Greek Old Testament to translate the Hebrew *Yahweh Elohim.* Jesus and Yahweh were equated in some way.

A number of texts could be adduced to illustrate the close community between Jesus and the Father, the preexistence of the Son, the distinctiveness of his human nature, and other aspects that would ground the later definitions of the Councils. But we must always remember that the Scriptures were speaking a different language with different concepts than were the Fathers and Doctors of the later Church. What can be shown is that there is a valid continuity between the two usages.

A good example of the early Church's belief in the lordship of Jesus can be seen in the following passage:

Because of this,
God highly exalted him
and bestowed on him the name
above every other name,
so that at Jesus' name
every knee must bend
in the heavens, on the earth
and under the earth,
and every tongue proclaim
to the glory of God the Father:
JESUS CHRIST IS LORD
(Philippians 2:9-11).

Exalted on High

How did the young Christian Church make the step from a recognition of Jesus of Nazareth as a wonder-worker and preacher of the Kingdom to a confession of him as Lord? It could only have been occasioned by the firm conviction that he had been exalted on high by the power of the Father. What he had done on earth was now consummated in glory. His terrestrial "authority" was given cosmic dimensions.

The event that sounded this proclamation of. lordship by the Father was the resurrection. That is why the resurrection is so inescapably central to the Christian faith. But just what is meant by resurrection? The theologians have written extensively on this subject in recent years. One commonly

accepted conclusion is that it is not to be equated
with the resuscitation of a corpse, as in the cases of
the son of the widow of Naim or of Lazarus. Jesus
did not return to *this* life with all the restrictions of
mortal life except that of mortality itself. Rather,
he was raised to a new kind of existence that made
it possible for him to exercise lordship in an unlim-
ited manner. This is clearly the conviction of the
early Christians in all of the references to the exalted Lord in the New Testament writings.

We would have to say, then, that those early
Christians who experienced the risen Jesus did not
experience the same kind of physical body that
they had known during his earthly existence. As
noted above, he did not have the same limitations
of that existence. That is what St. John implies
when he writes of the coming of Jesus in the apostles' midst "despite the locked doors" (John
20:26).

On the other hand, it cannot be said either that
the appearances of Jesus were simply the subjective mystical experiences of those involved. This
has been asserted in the past and is still asserted by some who cannot accept a glorified
transformation of Jesus that would establish the
grounds for his lordship. It has been shown that
the language used in the Gospels to describe the
resurrection appearances is not the language of
mystical experience. It is, instead, the ordinary
concrete language of everyday human encounters.
Moreover, this interpretation leaves unexplained
the tradition of the empty tomb, a tradition that
could have been easily confuted by the opponents

of the early Christians if it were not true.

Finally, those bizarre explanations that would suggest something like a successful ministering by close friends of Jesus after he was carried to the tomb near the point of death are hardly worth serious consideration. As Father Peter Riga has written, "Recent theories to explain the resurrection of Jesus, e.g., *The Passover Plot,* are nothing more than embellishments of former theories which have long since been discredited. The fact that they are today sensational and put between slick covers does not change that fact" (*The Bible Today,* April, 1971, p. 351).

The resurrection of Jesus is at the heart of the mystery of Christianity. There will never be an explanation that will completely satisfy those, either friends or foes, who are searching for "plain facts." If it were just a "plain fact" that could be verified by the scientific historian in the same way as any other fact of history, then it would have to be accepted by reason, not by faith; the mystery would be dissolved. Also, the lordship of Jesus would be reduced to a subjective experience of the "believer" with no basis in reality. It is difficult, if not impossible, to imagine Christianity surviving for two thousand years if its central message were but a subjective experience. The resurrection and lordship of Jesus are realities that cannot be separated.

This most intimate connection between Jesus' resurrection and his lordship is clearly attested to in the New Testament writings. In the Acts of the Apostles we find what is probably an early expression of it. The scene is that of Pentecost Sunday. Peter is explaining to the Jewish pilgrims to Jerusalem the meaning of the religious phenomenon they had just experienced. Having quoted the Old Testament prophecy about the coming of the Spirit upon all men in the messianic times, he says of Jesus, "This is the Jesus God has raised up, and we are his witnesses. Exalted at God's right hand, he first received the promised Holy Spirit from the Father, then poured this Spirit out on us. This is what you see and hear. . . . Therefore let the whole house of Israel know beyond any doubt that God has made both Lord and Messiah this Jesus whom you crucified" (2:32-36).

A remarkably similar statement is made by St. Paul in the opening words of his letter to the Romans. He writes that Jesus Christ "was made Son of God in power according to the spirit of holiness, by his resurrection from the dead: Jesus Christ our Lord" (1:4). The fact that we have two independent witnesses testifying to the same reality leaves little doubt of the early Church's association of resurrection and lordship.

These explicit testimonies are reinforced by many implied testimonies throughout the New Testament. We have already seen the passage from Paul's letter to the Philippians where Jesus is said to be exalted on high and given the name of Lord. Again, exaltation (resurrection) and lordship are associated.

Before the Resurrection

We learn from the Scriptures that it was only

through the resurrection from the dead that Jesus' lordship was recognized and made operative. But what about *before* the resurrection? Is there no connection between the early Christian's belief in Jesus' lordship and the historical Jesus of Nazareth? Certainly the early Christians would not have hesitated in their reply. The very fact that the early Church could write about the Lord Jesus in the context of a biography as they did in the Gospels shows that they identified the Lord they confessed with the Nazarean. But was this identification the *creation* of the Easter faith? Or does it have any roots in the man from Galilee—in his deeds? In what he said about himself?

All the evidence from the Gospels, and especially from that of Mark, suggests that Jesus' appearance among his countrymen and his message to them produced consternation, bewilderment, misunderstanding, hostility and, on the part of some, dedicated loyalty. In this sense we can say that the general atmosphere projected in *Jesus Christ, Superstar* reflects the Gospel tradition with some accuracy. His contemporaries did not know who Jesus was. Everything about him eluded their ability to give him a place in the everyday life of first-century Judaism.

Chief among these bewildering factors was his message and the sense of authority with which he preached it. The Gospels tell us that the message centered on the Kingdom of God (Mark 1:15). This was something the Jews could handle without difficulty. They knew about and eagerly awaited the coming of his Kingdom, for that would mean the

74

peace- and justice-filled reign of the God of Israel. Yahweh was Lord over his people and indeed over all nations and he would one day effectively establish his reign in the whole world. The expectation of that reign, of that lordship, was not only central to the Jewish faith; it had reached fever pitch at the time of Jesus. The message of the Kingdom of God was not new to Jesus' contemporaries.

What really bewildered them was the authority with which this Jesus preached the message and the sense of immediacy that he gave to it. So insistent was he on this immediacy that he frankly admitted he was bringing division among his people. The way he spoke about the Kingdom being present in their midst (cf. Luke 17:21) was bound to produce contrasting reactions: "Do not suppose that my mission on earth is to spread peace. My mission is to spread, not peace, but division. I have come to set a man at odds with his father, a daughter with her mother, a daughter-in-law with her mother-in-law: in short, to make a man's enemies those of his own household" (Matthew 10:34-36).

We have every reason to believe that this is an authentic saying of Jesus. It would be difficult, to say the least, to imagine the early Christians creating a saying like this about their Lord. That it was preserved at all can only be explained on the supposition that the early Church was persuaded Jesus had said it. And the only reason he would have said it is because he was fully aware of the radical nature of his message of the Kingdom. But it was not just the Kingdom; it was *his connection with the Kingdom.* There was the rubbing point.

Jesus had said to those who accused him of casting out devils by Beelzebub, "But if it is by the finger of God that I cast out devils, then the reign of God is upon you" (Luke 11:20). Here is a clear indication of Jesus' awareness not only that he was acting in the power of God but also that through that action God's Kingdom was being established now in their midst. This was what gave the sense of immediacy to what he said. "All who looked on were amazed. They began to ask one another, 'What does this mean? A completely new teaching in a spirit of authority'" (Mark 1:27).

Biblical scholars have shown that at the time of Jesus the Jewish people had a strong sense of both the past and the future. The past was the time of Yahweh's mighty deeds in favor of his people and, because of that, it was the past of promise. It pointed to a time when the promise inherent in God's covenant love for his people would be realized in a surpassing moment. It was that past which made the future the object of undying hope. In such a context the present was little more than a way-station between past and future, a time to be endured until the day of Yahweh would be manifested.

But it was this present that Jesus made the focus of his message. "The immediate present is the hallmark of all the words of Jesus, of his appearance and his actions, in a world which had lost the present. . . . Every one of the scenes described in the Gospels reveals Jesus' astounding sovereignty in dealing with situations according to the kind of people he encountered. . . . The Gospels call this patent immediacy of Jesus' sovereign power his 'authority.' The word 'authority' certainly contains already the mystery of Jesus' personality and influence, as understood by faith. It therefore transcends the merely 'historical' sphere. Yet it denotes a reality which appertains to the historical Jesus and is prior to any interpretation" (G. Bornkamm, *Jesus of Nazareth,* p. 60).

That Jesus exercised this kind of "authority" throughout his earthly life is the constant witness of the Gospels. His supreme decisiveness in choosing his disciples, his manifest freedom in interpreting the Law, his sweeping power over the forces of evil, his utter lack of embarrassment in dealing with sinners and society's outcasts, his royal dignity in the face of death—all were the fruit of his underlying "authority" and were recognized as such by his countrymen.

The World Is Not the Same

Let us review briefly what we have seen thus far. During his earthly ministry Jesus exercised what can be called a limited form of lordship. The Scriptures refer to this as his "authority." But that authority could not be exercised on a cosmic scale as long as he remained bound by the limitations of time and space. Only a liberation from these restrictions could place him in such a condition. Once that liberation had taken place through resurrection-exaltation, then Jesus was free to manifest his dominion and display his saving power for all. The sending of the Holy Spirit was the paramount expression of that power.

If there is confusion today about the divinity of Jesus, it can only be because the New Testament teaching about Jesus is not being taken seriously enough. When the early Christians made their confession that Jesus is Lord, and when Paul and the others recorded it in their writings, they were not offering a bit of interesting speculation for an elite group of philosophers. They were intending to be very real and very relevant. If Jesus *is* Lord, then the world just isn't the same as it was before he began exercising lordship. What is more, my role in life is going to be drastically affected by that same lordship of Jesus Christ. If he is Lord, then he has a claim on me, which obligates me to listen to his words and respond to them.

When the lordship of Jesus Christ is questioned or diminished in any way, the theology of mission is one of the first things to suffer. How can the missioner proclaim with any kind of dedicated zeal the Gospel message, the Good News of salvation, if the Lord of that salvation has been reduced to the rank of one more imposing figure in the outline of history? Any viable theology of Christian mission must take seriously that final charge of Jesus related in Matthew's Gospel: "Full authority has been given to me both in heaven and on earth; go, therefore, and make disciples of all the nations. Baptize them in the name of the Father, and of the Son, and of the Holy Spirit. Teach them to carry out everything I have commanded you. And know that I am with you always, until the end of the world" (28:18-20). Only the lordship of Jesus Christ gives

Christian mission its meaning and vitality.

The inner spiritual life of the Church and of individual members in the Church will also quickly deteriorate with the diminishing of Jesus' lordship. If we, as Christians, cannot find our identity through our relationship to the Lord Jesus Christ, then we call ourselves Christian in vain. "That is why I tell you that nobody who speaks in the Spirit of God ever says, 'Cursed be Jesus.' And no one can say: 'Jesus is Lord,' except in the Holy Spirit" (I Corinthians 12:3).

Questions for Discussion

1. Why is it easier for many people to accept Jesus as true God than to accept him as true man? Why is it that, today, emphasis seems to be almost exclusively on the humanity of Jesus?

2. Many people, disturbed by the emphasis on Jesus' humanity, ask: "Isn't Jesus God? Doesn't he have a divine nature? Isn't he the Second Person of the Blessed Trinity?" But what two difficulties does the author find with this type of question?

3. What is the basic Christian profession of faith?

4. What does the concept of lordship mean in the Old Testament? What are the unique qualities of Yahweh's lordship?

5. What does it mean when New Testament writers use the title *Kyrios* (Lord) when referring to Jesus in the same way that it was used of Yahweh in the Old Testament? In what sense is Jesus' divinity implied in his lordship?

6. Why is Jesus' lordship one of creative love rather than of oppression or restrictive domination?

7. How did the early Church make the step from a recognition of Jesus of Nazareth as a wonder-

worker and preacher of the Kingdom to a confession of him as Lord?

8. What was involved in the early Christians' experience of the risen Jesus? Why can't the resurrection be written off as a purely subjective experience?

9. Is there any connection between the early Christians' proclamation of the risen Jesus as Lord and their experience of him before the resurrection?

10. What does the author mean by Jesus' "limited lordship"?

11. Why is the question of Jesus' lordship a matter of immense practical concern rather than of theological speculation? What difference would it make in our lives if Jesus wasn't Lord?

Chapter V

The Kingdom Begun: Jesus As Moral Teacher

Kenneth D. Eberhard

There is a supposedly true story about an incident which occurred several years ago in an American Catholic seminary. As the young men were filing out of chapel after their evening prayers, they came across a drunken janitor sprawled across the corridor. One by one the seminarians stepped over the helpless man since there was a rule that they were to keep silence and not break ranks.

It is ironic, but we Christians can often ignore a central teaching of Jesus in order to follow only the outer edges of his doctrine. At times, in keeping the minimum requirements of his teaching we are unresponsive to the moral demand of the moment. We can insist on the letter of Jesus' "law" and at the same time violate the spirit of his life and teaching. The ancient traps into which the Pharisees fell are still our temptations today.

Jesus insisted that Christians are to be passionately concerned for the *truth*. All his biographers attest that this man, who once simply called himself "the truth," lived a life of utter honesty.

This simple peasant from Galilee lived fully as a man of his religion and his times, yet he never allowed his traditional upbringing in the law to shield him from new sources of truth. Jesus was obviously surprised at meeting a pagan centurion who seemed to have more faith than "all of Israel," but there he stood, and Jesus had only acceptance and praise. Pious Jews would scarcely look for the love of God in a common prostitute, but Jesus recognized it there and tried to call it to the attention of Simon and his refined guests.

Truths like these can be upsetting, Jesus recognized. The Pharisees were continually questioning him, trying to undermine the truthfulness of his message and teachings by pointing out how he failed to comply with the letter of Jewish law. They were scandalized when Jesus healed the paralytic on the Sabbath, because the law wouldn't allow it. But Jesus' approach was to measure laws by the truth, not the truth by laws, as was the Pharisees' bent. Jesus accepted reality as it came, trusting in the fathomless goodness of its Author. He had no pretenses to preserve, no "image" to save, no tradition to protect.

It is this openness to the truth which is the occasion for much confusion and difficulty in studying Jesus as a moral teacher. As human beings we crave security and never like to admit that we have been wrong. This seems to be particularly true in matters of religion. We, like the Pharisees, would prefer clear-cut rules and regulations so we can be *certain* that we are doing the will of God. Yet, as followers of Jesus, we must be pledged to the truth wherever it appears, even when there is no clear-cut Church law or saying of Jesus to back us up. We must be ready to respond generously to people and the situation even though there is no strict law commanding us to do so.

By continuing to study the Gospels anew, we can ever more deeply appreciate the Person of Jesus and the spirit of truth which characterized his life. As we come to a fuller understanding of his teaching and his central message, we will be better able to orientate our own lives in this same truthful direction.

The Teachings of Jesus

What precisely are the moral teachings of Jesus and what relevance do they have for us today? Can we go to the Scriptures to find solutions to today's moral problems of war, racism, divorce, abortion? Without question, Jesus made many moral decisions which the Gospel writers have passed on to us as important for our own Christian lives. In addition, he left us a number of parables which embody his moral viewpoint. Nonetheless, it remains a very difficult and complex task to apply these decisions and parables to our own lives today.

Jesus told Mary that she had chosen the better part and that Martha was wrong in asking her to help with the housework. Does this mean that

85

housewives today should pray rather than prepare dinner? To Judas, Jesus said that it was better that his feet be anointed with a costly perfume than that the ointment be sold for the sake of the poor. Does this justify expensive church furnishings in the face of world poverty? Jesus forbade a man who wished to become a disciple to return to bury his father. Does this mean the same for us today?

The simple truth of the matter is that the moral decisions of Jesus were always made with particular circumstances in mind. It is therefore almost impossible to take any individual saying of Jesus and automatically apply it to our own lives. The moral teachings of Jesus provide no "laws" as we are accustomed to understand this term. The "law of Christ" (i.e., love) is a dynamic principle; it is an attitude for living rather than a detailed code of behavior. This does not mean, however, that as a moral teacher Jesus has nothing to say to us.

By his life Jesus shows us what it is to love God and men. While not trying to copy slavishly his individual actions, we can perceive general "orientations" which are specifically Christian. Jesus shows us how a transformed personality expresses itself, and he challenges us to be as relevant to our situation as he was to his. It is vital, therefore, that Christians study the moral teachings of Jesus in order to discern the general directions which must be taken if we are to live a life of Christian love.

The great Christian theologian, Karl Barth, felt that we could discern six distinctive traits of morality as taught by Jesus:

• In many passages which treat of material possessions, a careful reader can see that Jesus is telling his followers that they cannot let money enslave them. Jesus speaks about how difficult it is for the rich to enter heaven. He calls the man a "fool" who is tearing down his barn to build a bigger one, for that very night his death shall occur. Through these and other stories Jesus teaches us that Christian love means not allowing wealth to control our lives. We must ever remain free to share our possessions with others.

• Another concrete Christian direction can be found by examining the texts which speak of becoming servants, of taking the last place at the table, of not competing for dignity. By these accounts, Jesus teaches us that Christian love means a freedom from social status. When social dignity and importance cause us to overlook a need of our neighbor, Christians are to let them go.

• A third consistency in Jesus' teachings has to do with force. Here Jesus counsels us not to fear those who can only kill the body, but to trust our heavenly Father. Moreover, he rebuked James and John for wishing to use violence against a Samaritan town, and he commanded Peter to sheathe his sword. Through these and other events and parables we learn that the love which Jesus teaches is one which is strongly committed to solving human problems through peaceful means.

• A fourth Christian trait which emerges from the Gospels is the free acceptance of our life situation. Time and time again Jesus instructs his disciples that if they are to follow him, they must learn to carry their crosses. At the Last Supper he promised Christians that just as he was persecuted, so will we be. As society hated Jesus, so will it hate us. Far from assuring Christians that his way is an easy one, he explicitly tells us that we must learn to bear sufferings.

• The fifth characteristic of Jesus' moral teachings is his insistence upon a final freedom from family ties. We are actually told in Mark's Gospel that Jesus' own relatives came to stop his preaching since they judged him out of his mind. But Jesus would not be stopped. So, too, he emphasized that his family, in the deepest sense of the word, were those who did the will of his Father. Jesus, then, made it clear that blood ties are secondary to spiritual obligations. A Christian is one who must take his own freedom with absolute seriousness. It is not to his relatives that he is first accountable, and he may never let them turn him from what he knows to be right.

• The final "general pattern" of Jesus' moral teachings concerns our piety. Jesus insists that it be simple and never for the sake of show. When we fast, Jesus tells us to wash our face and anoint our heads so that only our heavenly Father knows of our fast. He states that a good place to pray is in the privacy of one's room. The display and arrogance of the Pharisee, who loudly proclaims how often he prays and how much he gives to the Temple, is strongly contrasted with the publican who, with eyes cast down, humbly admits his sins and begs forgiveness.

By not focusing on any one teaching or statement of Jesus, but rather by taking them as a group, we are able to discern the general orientations of Jesus' teachings and begin in some way to apply them to our own life situation. We can begin to ask such questions as: How can I become less violent and more of a peacemaker in my relations with others? How can I test my own and my family's detachment from material possessions?

As effective as this approach might be, however, there remains a deeper level at which we can understand Jesus as moral teacher.

The Message of Jesus

Much is written today about "the message of Jesus." What does this mean? A message tends to be something short and clipped: something we are perhaps expecting, and when it comes we are able to order other events around it. When we ask about the moral teachings of Jesus, we are asking a very complex question which involves a search for a coherent and systematic presentation of moral truths. But when we inquire about whether Jesus had a message, we are looking for something simple and more basic. Moreover, if Jesus did have a message and we discover it, then we are at once in a position to gain a much deeper understanding of his teaching.

Jesus definitely did have a message and we are told quite clearly what it is. In the first chapter of his Gospel, Mark gives us the overall theme of Jesus' preaching: "The time has come and the Kingdom of God is close at hand. Reform your lives and believe in the Good News" (1:15).

Jesus' message is a call to conversion because the Kingdom of God is near. In a very simple and straightforward way, he called his followers to make a basic decision in favor of God and his eternal love. He told us that if we wish, God is making it possible for us to transcend our own selfishness and to become a "man for others."

As John the Evangelist saw so clearly, the way in which we are called to love God is to love our brothers. No man can love God and at the same time hate his brother. One of the most powerful sermons of Jesus concerns the Last Judgment where the elect are rewarded by the King and told that it is because they fed, clothed, visited and cared for him. This comes to them as a total surprise and they quite simply ask, "Lord, when did we see you hungry and feed you . . ." (Matthew 25:37). The reply is equally simple, and quite compelling: "I tell you the plain truth, inasmuch as you did this to one of these least brethren of mine you did it to me" (25:40).

Jesus' message is to see each moment as a time of opportunity, an occasion of grace, whereby we can love the Father anew by loving our brother. Jesus, then, summoned us to conversion: a new attitude whereby we are ready in each moment to decide once more to transcend ourselves in service of the neighbor.

Catholic moral theologians Bernard Haring and Charles Curran draw a number of very fruitful reflections from this basic message of conversion. They first of all point out that the message calls us to believe in the Good News: it is a proclamation of joy. While fully acknowledging the presence of evil in the world, Jesus could nevertheless maintain a mature attitude of joy and optimism in the goodness of his Father.

These Catholic theologians also stress how fortunate we are that the Gospel-writer Matthew decided to present a condensation of the teachings of Jesus and thus gathered them together into one "sermon" which quite distinctively emphasizes his message. Even though St. Luke locates the historical core of this sermon on a piece of level ground, Matthew situates it on a mountain. This may be because he understands Jesus as promulgating a "New Law." Thus, just as Moses proclaimed the Old Law from Mount Sinai, so too is Jesus presented on a mountain as Matthew condenses the teaching of Jesus into one sermon. We know it today as the Sermon on the Mount.

The Sermon begins with nine proclamations of joy. We call these statements the Beatitudes and have normally translated each one as beginning with the word *blessed* (e.g., "Blessed are the poor in spirit, theirs is the kingdom of heaven"). However, the Greek word which begins each statement can also be translated, as *happy*. Thus the renowned Jerusalem Bible reads, "How *happy* are the poor in spirit. . . ." Moreover, as if in summary of these nine proclamations of joy, Jesus ends them by saying, "Rejoice and be glad, for your reward will be great in heaven" (5:12).

Matthew then advances into the New Law's teachings. The Law of Moses forbade killing, but

Jesus forbids anyone to even become angry. The Old Law condemned adultery; Jesus condemns even the adulterous desire. Moses allowed divorce; Jesus does not. The Old Law prescribed fidelity to oaths, while the Christian New Law excludes any swearing whatsoever: "All you need say is 'Yes' if you mean yes, 'No' if you mean no" (5:37). The Old Testament treated justice according to the Law of Talion: an eye for an eye, a tooth for a tooth. Jesus commands his followers to abstain from all violence and to offer no resistance whatsoever. If you are struck on the cheek, then turn the other. If you are sued for part of your possessions, hand over everything. If you are forced to walk one mile, walk two. Moreover, never refuse to lend money to anyone. Finally, Jesus tells his followers that they will have to love even their enemies and pray for their persecutors. In a word, they must be perfect just as their heavenly Father is perfect.

Even though the Sermon on the Mount appears to be a series of new teachings, we think that it is more insightfully understood as an elaboration of Jesus' message. This is because Jesus' "laws" or "teachings" are really impossible for human beings on their own power to keep perfectly at all times. Who of us is able never to become angry, or never refuse to lend money, or never entertain a lustful thought? What is being presented here is the basic demand of the Kingdom of God: a Kingdom which Jesus announces but whose fulfillment is still a future event.

The Sermon on the Mount sets down "goal commandments": a perfection toward which every

Christian should strive according to his abilities. They are not meant as inviolable laws. There are times when we must refuse to lend money, when we cannot help but become selfishly angry, when we must back up our words with an oath. But it is important that the Christian realize that in doing so he is failing to realize the fullness of the Kingdom. No matter what the Christian does, he continually falls short. (This is a sobering thought to anyone who hoped to achieve salvation on his own merits by fulfilling all the laws.)

When Jesus talks about conversion, therefore, he is not referring to a single event but to an ongoing reality in our lives. Since conversion is in the context of the radical demand of the Kingdom, it is really a call to continual growth. This indeed is what is meant by Christian love. Love is that reality which only remains itself when it is surpassing itself. A person not open to achieving a greater love really has no love at all.

When Jesus met the rich young man and heard that he had kept the law perfectly from his youth, he approved of this but then gave him a radical demand of selling everything he possessed. The young man went away saddened (Luke 18:18-23). The command was too much for him and he realized that he really was not living his moral possibilities to the fullest and that he had a long way to go before he would. (The law, in itself, does not save us.) His life, then, could no longer be complacent and his conscience was no longer free from tension. Had he been able to sell all his possessions and follow Jesus, one feels sure that Jesus would have required something else which was beyond him and thus again placed him in the tension of the radical demand.

Catholic moral theology has probably focused too much attention on the teachings of Jesus and has overlooked the dynamic importance of his message. Our ethics have often been too cut and dried, too rationalistically clear, thereby deadening our awareness of Jesus' radical demand. In the name of a doctrine of "just war," we have allowed ourselves to experience none of the tension of war's raw horror. Jesus' message of the Kingdom with its "radical demand" and "goal commandment" were forgotten and we too easily gave up our Christian bias towards pacifism.

This is the result of the persistent human temptation to Pharisaism—to reduce morality to easily measurable behavior. Once we do this we no longer experience the pushing and prodding of the Spirit toward a greater discovery and living out of the truth in our lives. We have rationalized Jesus' message down to size so that it no longer seriously challenges us.

On the other hand, we sometimes go to the opposite extreme. By elevating a "goal commandment" into an absolute, we forget that it is something to be sought after but, because of the human sin-filled situation, cannot always be obtained. Thus, in the name of a doctrine of sacramental marriage, we have shielded ourselves from the problems of the intolerable marriage and the deserted partner. Many times we have refused to consider a divorce when the situation actually seemed to call for granting one.

Another false response to the radical demand of Jesus' message is to become discouraged when faced with the impossibility of perfection. In this case, as with the two responses described above, we are unable to accept and live with the ambiguity of the truth.

In order to shirk the constant demands that Jesus' message makes on us, we insist that laws be cast in such a way that the possibility of fulfilling them is insured, or we insist on enforcing an absolute in such an unloving manner that no one involved is healed by Jesus' message, or we give up from the outset in discouragement.

We must never forget that the message of Jesus is a message of tension: the Kingdom has begun but it is not yet fulfilled. Insofar as the Kingdom is now underway we must idealistically strive for its completion. Insofar as it is not yet fulfilled, we must realistically deal with the world as it actually is, and this means coming to terms with the sin-filled situation. Paradoxically, it is when one constantly lives with the *tension* of striving for the ideal set by Jesus that he knows the *peace* which only Jesus can give. The tension is not psychological anxiety or always being on edge, but the demand of love always to be open to the unexpected challenge of the present moment or situation.

The Gospels show us that Jesus became angry with only two groups of people: the Pharisees and the rich. Each group is characterized by a type of security and absence of tension. The Pharisees, because they have the law and keep it to the letter, illustrate a smugness which Jesus finds repugnant. Likewise he proclaims that the rich will only be saved with difficulty because they have so little an awareness of their own need. Both groups need a realization that the Kingdom has begun but is not yet fulfilled. They need the tension proclaimed in Jesus' message.

There remains, however, a third and yet deeper level at which one can understand Jesus as moral teacher. Moreover, it is at this level that we can perceive how Jesus' moral teaching differs from that of all other philosophies and religions.

The Spirit of Jesus

Above we have spoken briefly about Jesus' moral teachings and his message. Before proceeding further, we should honestly ask ourselves "Have they really made any difference?" Are Christians and Christian cultures any more moral than peoples of other religious beliefs, or even agnostics and atheists?

The great Christian moral theologian Reinhold Niebuhr warned against trying to verify historically any moral superiority of the Christian faith. Century after century shows that Christians have succumbed to the temptations of the age just as readily as anyone else. In his study on racial prejudice in the United States, Gordon Allport reported that churchgoers tended to be more racially biased than those who did not attend worship services. The religious sociologist Thomas O'Dea thinks that American Catholics as a group are even more materialistic than the average U.S. citizen. This, he feels, explains why we produce more than our share of doctors and lawyers yet fall short in our percentage of college professors and teachers. Finally, the great impetus for world justice and the redistribution of wealth does not seem to be coming today from Christianity but from atheistic Communism. It is said that one of the highest compliments a Latin American can pay to a clergyman is to call him "a Communist priest," which is their way of saying "a priest who is concerned about social reform and the poor."

What difference then does Christian morality make? This difficult and even embarrassing question can only be understood if we take our discussion one level deeper. It is not enough to concentrate on either the teachings of Jesus or his message. If we are to grasp fully the meaning of Jesus as moral teacher, then we must recognize that we are not primarily talking about information or even a proclamation of the Kingdom. Rather, in the last analysis, we must be talking about Jesus' continuing presence.

Jesus as moral teacher cannot be separated from the doctrine of his resurrection. For Christians, Jesus is not someone who lived 2,000 years ago and left us some remarkable teachings about love. No, he is alive today and present to the world through his Spirit.

This continuing presence of Jesus is what primarily distinguishes Christianity from other religious and ethical systems. The Buddha, Confucius, and Socrates are important primarily for their teachings. But Jesus is important principally for his risen presence in the world today. If it were only his teachings which held Christians together, then we could quite honestly judge that we could do better with a teacher who speaks more directly to our times such as Albert Camus, Mahatma Gandhi, Dag Hammarskjold or Martin Luther King.

Thus St. Thomas Aquinas, when he discusses the character of the New Law as distinct from the Old, says that the New Law is not something which is primarily written. No, "the New Law consists chiefly in the grace of the Holy Spirit. . . . Now men become receivers of this grace through God's Son made man, whose humanity grace filled first, and thence flowed forth to us. . . . Of his fullness we have all received, and grace for grace. Hence it is added that grace and truth came by Jesus Christ" (I, IIae, Q.108, 1 c). For St. Thomas, therefore, the moral teaching of Jesus is primarily given to us in the presence of the Holy Spirit.

We have only to recall one further point and our picture is complete. We are thinking of the Christian doctrine that God wills all men to be saved, whether they have heard of Christ or not. If this be true, and if the only way in which God is present to man is in Christ, then Jesus must be present in his Spirit to all men. Just as all men use the rules of logic whether they have learned them or not, so do all men use the guidance of Jesus regardless of whether they have learned that this inner voice who guides them is his.

This is not to say that it is unimportant whether one hears the written teachings and message of Jesus. Something can be unnecessary and still be important. It is not necessary to be literate in order to be human, yet who would say that literacy is unimportant? Properly used, literacy is a great help to the development of our humanity. Likewise, properly grasped, the teachings and message of Jesus are a great help to the development of our Christian life. But the one thing necessary is his presence to us in his Spirit, and in this all mankind shares.

Father Charles Curran has written, "Only a naive biblicism would expect to find in the Scriptures the solutions to the problems confronting man and society today. The ethical teaching of Jesus urges his followers to creatively find solutions to come to the aid of the neighbor who is in need." We cannot use the Bible as an answer book. The most that can be discerned from its teachings are certain prominent directions. More fruitful is the taking to heart of the message of Jesus. The "radical demand" of his Kingdom shows us that we can never do enough and must continually grow in love and creativity.

At its deepest level, however, the moral teaching of Jesus is his risen presence to us in the Spirit. This is why the proclamation of the Christian moral life is also a proclamation of joy. We rejoice that his Spirit is not just the prerogative of those who confess Jesus with their lips. Every man, to use the expressions of Teilhard de Chardin, lives in a "Divine Milieu" and is involved in a process of "Christogenesis."

And this is also why the moral teachings of

Jesus necessarily involve the Church. For we are not speaking primarily of something which happened 2,000 years ago but something which is happening in the Christian "now." Thus when Christians come together to reflect critically upon what Jesus is asking of us today, we profess that he is guiding us with his Spirit. An individual Christian can and must arrive at moral decisions, but he should always be concerned about consulting with other Christians, since we know so well how our pride and selfishness lead to self-deceit. Thus the more Christians one consults, the better; and if Christians the world over come to a moral agreement, then we have the greatest certainty possible of what the Spirit is saying. Hence, the surest voice of the Spirit is the Church. Jesus as moral teacher speaks to us today through his Church.

That the individual moral decisions of Jesus cannot be copied by us today may be looked upon by some as a loss. However, when we consider the general patterns which emerge from his teachings, the power of his message of conversion, and the fact that his Spirit is present to us today, then we can see that Jesus as a moral teacher is of enormous significance to our daily lives. True, he does not give us individual answers to our moral problems. But he does give us "the way," "the door," and "the path"—and this is his living presence among us.

St. Augustine, whose experience in moral struggles is well known, felt deeply this presence of Jesus. In my opinion, he has one forceful statement which expresses his lived realization of Jesus' message and Spirit: "We are Easter men, and Alleluja is our song!"

Questions for Discussion

1. Why does the author say that we cannot use the Bible as an "answer book" to solve our moral problems? Why don't the moral teachings of Jesus provide us with "laws," as we are accustomed to understand this term?

2. In what ways was Jesus so open to the truth that he was a source of scandal to many of his fellow Jews? What would be involved in striving to develop a similar openness to moral truth in our own lives?

3. Give some examples of how a person, in order to keep the minimum requirements of Jesus' teachings can be unresponsive to the moral demands of the moment? Give some examples of how a person can so insist on the letter of Jesus' "law" that he violates the spirit of Jesus' life and teaching?

4. What are the six distinctive moral traits that can be discerned in Jesus' teaching? How can we use each of these as a basis for examining the moral direction of our own lives? As a basis for formulating our response to particular moral dilemmas?

5. What is the *message* of Jesus? What is the basic moral challenge contained in this message?

6. Why is the conversion which Jesus talks about an ongoing reality rather than a single event? What effect should the conversion process have on our whole approach to moral decision-making?

7. Why does the author say that Jesus' proclamations in the Sermon on the Mount are not "laws" but elaborations of Jesus' message?

8. What are meant by "goal commandments" and how do these help us understand the basic tension of Jesus' message?

9. How does the story of the rich young man in the Gospel serve as an example of the radical moral demands that are imposed on each of us by the Kingdom? What different forms might such moral demands take in different individuals' lives?

10. What does it mean to say that the message of Jesus is a message of tension? How might an individual, aware of this tension, try to think through,

in his own life, the morality of divorce or birth control or participation in the Vietnam war?

11. What are the pitfalls we must avoid if we are to keep ourselves open and responsive to the radical demands of Jesus' message?

12. What groups of people did Jesus become angry with in the Gospel? Why? What aspects of our own lives might provoke this same kind of anger?

13. What primarily distinguishes Christianity from other religious and ethical systems?

14. If Jesus is present in the Spirit to all men, then why is it important whether one hears the actual message and teachings of Jesus?

15. Why do the moral teachings of Jesus necessarily involve the Church? What role should the Church play in an individual Christian's process of moral decision-making?

Chapter VI

Jesus In My Life

The following nine people of diverse backgrounds were interviewed about the presence and meaning of Jesus in their lives.

Johnny Cash, popular country singer, recently completed a movie about the life of Jesus.

Why do you believe in Jesus?

That's probably the hardest question of all because I don't understand *not* believing in Jesus. He's such an important part of my life. I call on him when I need advice. The Spirit of Jesus is always there, and he guides me. I can't say *why* I believe in Jesus. I just do it as something that is built into me.

Have you always believed in Jesus?

For as long as I can remember. Jesus and the Gospel have been an important part of my life from childhood. I grew up on a farm in northeastern Arkansas. The first songs I can remember singing were hymns and spirituals—songs about Jesus and songs about the Holy Land. I always wanted to go to Israel because that was where Jesus lived. As a child I longed to walk the places where he walked and see the things that were familiar to him in his childhood. And I was finally able to do that while making my movie on Jesus.

How has believing in Jesus affected your life?

Jesus is the foundation of my whole life. He is my strength. If you have Jesus in your life, you know it, you feel it. He's the solid rock you can stand on every day. There's no problem you can't face if you have the love of Jesus to strengthen you.

I know Jesus is alive in my life. My wife and I try to live our daily lives according to the teachings of Jesus. We have tried to study the Scriptures to know what road to take in particular circumstances. In many ways his Gospel is complicated, but as far as daily living it is so simple—it's a question of right and wrong, good and bad. Man is born with free will and can make choices. He's the only animal in God's kingdom that has free will. We have the right to choose daily between right and wrong.

Where might we find Jesus if he walked among us today?

As Jesus said many times, his Kingdom was not of this world. He did not come as an earthly Messiah to set up an earthly Kingdom. The Kingdom he represented was the Kingdom of love in the hearts of men and women. So far as I can get it out of the Scriptures, he didn't care one way or the other about earthly governments.

So I think if Jesus were alive today on this earth, you wouldn't find him at the White House arguing politics or in any kind of earthly social demonstrations.

What do you think of the present-day Jesus movement?

It's not a fad. It's here to stay. No matter how people today are looking for him, they are going to find him. Once he gets into your heart, he's there to stay.

What about *Jesus Christ, Superstar*?

I think it might be good entertainment, and I intend to see it when I get the chance. But I don't think I could possibly take it seriously as a story about Jesus because it ends with his death. Any story about Jesus has to show him resurrected or we cannot take it seriously. Without the resurrection of Jesus, we have no religion.

Dorothy Day

Dorothy Day, a convert from Communism to Catholicism, is the co-founder of the Catholic Worker movement and founder-editor of the Catholic Worker *newspaper.*

Why do you believe in Jesus?

I began to believe in Jesus when I came across a

Bible. I felt the holiness of the book in my hands. The Bible has a profound effect on me. The Word in the Bible is like the Word made flesh. It has a power—you can't explain why. It's like when you read a book and you suddenly recognize the truth there.

You can't explain faith. It's just a beautiful gift that suddenly comes, unasked and undeserved.

What does Jesus mean to you?

The two hardest sayings of Jesus are "Do not judge" and "Forgive them, they know not what they do." These mean that we cannot go ahead

with our righteous indignation and righteous wrath. Of course, we have to make judgments, but somehow we must avoid judging people personally.

To judge means not to have compassion, and compassion means "suffering with." So we must share in the passion of Christ and share in the suffering of all men. We must "suffer with" people, not judge them.

It's so easy to make judgments. People judge the poor when they complain, "We pay taxes to support their laziness." But Jesus says, "Do not judge." Don't judge this pregnant girl who is going to have an abortion, even though you try to persuade her not to. Don't judge the person who is a victim of alcoholism. Don't judge the soldier who thinks he is doing the right thing by killing.

This is a peculiar thing about Christianity — this insistence that we not judge. Of course we make judgments about the practicalities of living and we make judgments about ideas in general. But we cannot judge people.

This is not a simple thing to do. The only thing that gives us any light at all is to pray. And the simple prayers from the Gospel are best: "Lord, that I may see."

How do you experience Jesus in your own life?

I think that everyone who has gone through a religious conversion feels that they have been saved by Jesus. We have knowledge of salvation by the forgiveness of our sins. I think it's a wonderful feeling to have the slate wiped clean. And you can just keep starting over again — every morning, in fact.

"I have just begun," is the motto of some religious orders. I think there is a knowledge or experience of salvation there.

And because we are really children of one Father, we can be secure. There's a real sense of security, a real feeling of sureness about that. And so we don't have to brood about our lives.

What do you say about Jesus to the young people who come to your hospitality house and to your farm?

I don't talk about Jesus at all. I don't think that people should go around preaching that way. By our work and by our lives we give witness.

Although I was not brought up with talk of Jesus or religion, I learned by my parents' lives of goodness. As Peter Maurin said, "Be what you want other people to be."

One young fellow came up to me and said, "Do you believe in the divinity of Christ?" All I could say was, "I believe." You cannot explain it.

Of course at times we do burst out and talk about Jesus. We don't do it to preach, but rather because we are reminded of him by something. For instance, you start judging and you suddenly remember that Jesus said, "Do not judge."

What do you think about the current interest in Jesus in pop culture?

I think the enthusiasm for prayer and for the supernatural seen in houses for prayer, in the Pentecostal movement and in the Jesus freaks, as they call themselves, reveals the craving of the human heart in this barren civilization of ours. These young people have a desire for the folly of the cross and a sense of the two sides of the coin: cross and resurrection, suffering and rejoicing. I think that's a great discernment on the part of the young.

And so all this present emphasis on the mystical and the supernatural is intensely interesting, but it shouldn't lead us to forget the Incarnation. We have to put flesh on our spirituality.

Jesus shows us what this means in the 25th chapter of Matthew's Gospel in the parable of the Last Judgment: ". . . for I was hungry and you gave me food. . . ." I guess what animated us at the Catholic Worker is this idea that unless we clothe the naked, feed the hungry, shelter the harborless, visit the imprisoned and the sick, bury the dead, we are going to be judged.

I think the commune movement among young people is a move in the right direction. They are beginning to get a grasp of how to *incarnate* their ideas and ideals.

Kenneth Woodward

Kenneth Woodward, a graduate of the University of Notre Dame, is the religion editor of Newsweek *magazine.*

What does Jesus mean to you?

As a religion editor I can't help but be very conscious that there are many kinds of Jesuses for many kinds of people. In a sense, by their Jesus you will know them.

111

I've been a Roman Catholic all my life, and my
Jesus comes to me through that tradition. So I
have a rather different sort of Jesus as a result of
this than if, say, I had been a Southern Baptist. As
a Roman Catholic you experience many Jesuses:
the Baby Jesus in the crib at Christmas times,
Jesus in the host, Jesus as God.

The Incarnation is at the core of the Catholic
sensibility, and when the divinity of Christ is emphasized to the point of distortion, a balance must
be sought. Roman Catholic thinkers are doing this
now, and I am among those for whom a stress on
his humanity comes as a much needed corrective.
As I look at Jesus now, I try to understand him first
as a man like me. In fact, I would venture to say
that no one really can understand what it means to
be divine, except by very weak analogy. Jesus
doesn't tell us. He tells us what it means to be
truly human. Concretely, existentially, sacramen-
tally, I don't think we can approach divinity except through *his* humanity.

What aspects of the human Jesus are the most meaningful for you personally?

Over the years his words on the cross are the ones
that I have come most to appreciate: "My God, my
God, why have you forsaken me?" I feel if Jesus
can feel hung up and forsaken and uncertain in
that sense—and he's Jesus—then what about me?
How can I be so certain—certain in the sense of
being so secure? So I tend to think of a Jesus who
has had some sense of being one with the Father,
who had to grow in knowledge, and who was being

led down a path, the end of which he couldn't see all that clearly.

I also see Jesus as a teacher who tended to turn things inside out through his Gospel stories. For example, there was extant in his time a parable of the prodigal son. But who's the hero of the prodigal son story as Jesus tells it? Not the prodigal son, but the father who accepts him. The father could have said, "I've got my other son and he didn't leave me, but this one did." But he sees him in the distance and begins to make ready a feast. Now it is incomprehensible to me that someone would act this way. And now that I am a father I know how I might feel under those circumstances—that if one of my kids runs off I'm not about to turn around and do that. But I also know that if I am going to buy this Jesus thing, then that story reflects how I'm *supposed* to act.

What other demands does believing in Jesus make on your life?

The religion of Jesus is certainly a religion with suffering at the core. And I'm not at all certain that I want to suffer. But I know that if I am going to be a Christian I must learn to suffer—and repent of sins I am all too willing to ignore.

This doesn't mean that one goes out and puts one's head on the block or that one ceases to alleviate suffering. The thing is, though, the more sensitive to people you become, the more you are going to suffer. The more you eradicate the obvious kinds of suffering, the more you find subtle kinds of suffering. I'm not so sure I want to do it. I've got

to convince myself over and over again that I want
to be a Christian.

**Do you feel that you have had any personal ex-
periences of Jesus in your life?**

Yes, but I see them as "mediated" by my mem-
bership in a specific American Catholic subcul-
ture. Besides, I am immensely distrustful of people
who feel that they have had a personal experience
of Jesus. The reason I am skeptical is that I've met
too many of these people who claim to have had an
experience of Jesus, and they don't strike me as
very Christian—or pleasant. They have the tendency to feel saved—already sitting in the lap of
the Lord as a result of their experience.

I suspect I have developed a bias against a religion that tries to focus on or prepare you for a do-
or-be-damned encounter, whether it's on the way
to Damascus, on the way to church or at a charis-
matic revival meeting. That's not my thing and I
think that comes partly because I was born into a
sacramental tradition. The Catholic tradition says
that you encounter Christ in everyday things like
bread and wine, like the marriage bed, like in my
brother. It is in these very human things that one
finds oneself and finds Christ.

And so, as much as I admit to liking an elevat-
ed sense of coziness with Christ, I think I will keep
my nose to the ground and go with the prosaic. I
think that I will go with the bread and wine, the
everyday experiences. I won't necessarily wait for
—though I would certainly welcome—the personal
experience. I prefer to be surprised by grace.

Gail Dunfey, 21, is the youngest of nine members on the city council of Lowell, Massachusetts. After high school she spent two years in the Sisters of Notre Dame de Namur.

Why do you believe in Jesus?

Because of my Catholic family background there has always been a God-figure in my life. But this only gradually developed into a personal relationship, with God becoming someone that I could talk to. It was in high school that I came to realize that God had something to say to me, and that I had to make a response to him. But it was only after I entered the convent that I became aware of the person of Jesus and began to develop a relationship with him. From then on it was through Jesus that I came to know the Father.

This is how my belief in Jesus developed over the years. But as for *why* I believe, that is a mystery. Faith is a mystery in anyone's life.

How do you think of Jesus?

I think of Jesus as a human being like myself. But we don't have to be exactly alike. I see myself as political, but I don't want to say, therefore, that Jesus was a politician or political revolutionary. I am cautious of making Jesus too much like myself.

Jesus was a sensitive human being, always available to others. He allowed other people to affect his life, to change his life. And I think this is what is most important to me about Jesus—being able to let people affect my life.

Of course I believe that Jesus is God. But I have to realize that this is a mystery. And it's not that important to me to figure out how Jesus can be both man and God. I like to live with mystery.

What demands does Jesus make on you?

Jesus is always asking me to be open to reality as it is, to try to understand what love means. He demands that I take a lot of risks—the risk of being open to other people, of trusting people even when I am afraid to trust them. And this is hard. It brings with it a certain amount of insecurity. I know I am going to be misunderstood. I know there will be failures. All of this causes a lot of doubt in my life. If I didn't believe in Jesus, I wouldn't have the courage to take these risks.

117

The Good News of Jesus is hope. Because of him I know that what I am doing is not in vain. I have hope in knowing that Jesus lives.

How do you meet Jesus in your daily life?

I meet Jesus through prayer. I like to pray, and I like to pray with others when I have the chance. I need to take time out from my activity to make sure that Jesus is directing my life. I think we can fool ourselves into believing that Jesus is important to us and at the same time keep pushing him further and further aside.

I have just moved into my own apartment and I like living alone. It gives me time to reflect on what I'm doing. I think it's when I'm reflecting on *why* I make the decisions that I do that Jesus most affects my life.

What do you think about the contemporary Jesus movement?

My belief in Jesus is a very quiet one. I'm not a Jesus freak. I want to say something about Jesus by the kind of life I live, but I'm not interested in preaching about Jesus. I want to have the qualities of Jesus in my life, but maybe it's not important for people to know what inspires me.

I don't think that Jesus should ever be an escape from the problems around us. Believing in Jesus should make us active people, committed people. Yet from what I've seen, contemporary Jesus people seem to be using Jesus to provide a false sense of peace, a cure-all for the world's ills. It's as if they want the prize without running the race.

Gary MacEoin, journalist, editor, lawyer, reporter, lecturer, and university teacher, is the author of a weekly syndicated column on world affairs which appears in U.S. and Canadian Catholic newspapers.

What does Jesus mean to you?

I grew up in a very conventional Roman Catholicism, unquestioning and unchallenging. It offered me a Jesus who was primarily negative, that is, who was an indicator of what I should *not* do. This was a very individualistic and moralistic way of looking at Jesus.

Today I see Jesus primarily in positive terms. I think of him as a man who was literally a man of God, a man who was consciously aware of his relationship to a higher destiny and the role which God had identified for him as his purpose in life.

Through the Gospels and through my shared faith with others, I have come to acknowledge him to be the Son of God.

Therefore Jesus serves as a guide in all my decision-making. He is someone whose viewpoint I want to know so that I can adjust my own attitude on a particular issue and my own action accordingly. I recognize that I must join with him in building up the human community. All men, including myself, would want to approach the perfection of his commitment to what he called his "Father's business."

Why is believing in Jesus important?

I think it is important to first recognize what life would be like without belief in Jesus. Believers have tended excessively to regard nonbelievers as incapable of becoming equally involved in the creation of the world. I no longer think in those terms. What I do see as the difference between myself and a nonbeliever is our approach to creating a better world. The nonbeliever is obliged by principle to concentrate primarily on the notion of justice. Whereas the Christian is able to complement justice with the notion of love which he has seen incarnated in Jesus. The nonbeliever does not have this same exemplar of total love to whom he can turn. I think it is interesting to look at the attempts of Communists to build a better society. The means used tend to be inhuman means. This is reason operating without the application of the higher faculty of love, which Jesus always insisted on with his followers.

What would Jesus be like if he walked the earth today?

As I see it, he might be a member of a refugee family in Bengal or the Gaza Strip. Or he might be born into the family of a Wall Street stockbroker. But in either case, I see a repetition of the lifework of Jesus of the Gospel, that is to say, a life devoted to curing the sick, feeding the hungry, or as the Gospel expresses it, doing good. I suspect that the impact he would have would be confined to a relatively small and seemingly unimportant group of people, as was the impact of Jesus 2,000 years ago.

Mother Waddles

Mother Waddles, 59, has been called an "urban saint" by the mayor of her city, Detroit. The mother of 10 children, she is an ordained non-denominational minister who runs a 24-hour-a-day "Perpetual Mission" in Detroit's black ghetto.

Why do you believe in Jesus?

I believe in Jesus because I believe in the Holy Bible. I believe that the Bible was written by men who were inspired. My only sorrow today is that people are not still recording, because God is still working miracles.

How do you understand Jesus' message?

He taught us to love our neighbor as ourselves, to do unto others as we would have them do unto us, not to point a finger at someone and judge them.

121

He told us to love the young and the old, blacks and whites, the poor and the rich, Catholics, Protestants and Jews. He taught us to live with each other and love one another. Jesus taught us how to live, not die.

How does your belief in Jesus affect your daily life?

If I didn't believe in Jesus, I wouldn't be here. I've taken for the foundation of my mission the 25th chapter of St. Matthew: "When I was hungry, you fed me. . . ."

My work is really based on the philosophy that Jesus left for us. It's my contention that if the world is to be a better place to live and if God is to be magnified, then we who love Jesus must follow his principles and make them work here on earth.

I consider myself a demonstrator for God. I try to have the same mind in me that was in Jesus Christ, to let my light, my good works, shine—not to glorify me, but to glorify the Father.

What do you think of the contemporary Jesus people?

I think they are groping to find their way. But they need guidance. They need to sit down and study.

I tell young people that they must recognize that they are made in the image and likeness of God. The best way to tell people about Jesus is to have them recognize him in themselves.

Michael Cullen

Michael Cullen, one of the "Milwaukee Fourteen" arrested two years ago for burning draft records in Milwaukee, was released from prison a year ago. Since that time he has been living on a farm in northern Wisconsin with his wife, Netty, and their three children. An ex-seminarian, the 30-year-old Irish immigrant is the founder of Casa Maria, a Catholic Worker Hospitality House in Milwaukee.

What does Jesus mean to you?

Christ is the embodiment of the Word of God. He is God's image. Because of Jesus, the word of God is not abstract; it is flesh and bone. Incredible! You and I, individuals that have been converted to Christ, are called to become flesh and bone like him, to take on his word, to be what he was. That's a journey of a lifetime. And it all depends on God's grace and our openness to it.

How do you experience Jesus in your life today?

I feel him disturbing me. I think of Jesus as one who disturbs the very depths of my being. You cannot live in these times and say you're for Jesus when men and women are killing and murdering one another, because the Good News is a Gospel of peace. With our country involved in the Vietnam war, I couldn't see how I could be a part of the war and be a follower of Jesus. I wouldn't be able to consider myself at one with him. We have no choice but to be peacemakers.

And we followers of Jesus have to be about peacemaking at sacrifice to ourselves. Jesus' strong message comes through in the crucifixion as well as resurrection. The crucifix is so real, so vivid in the world today.

It is Jesus who would have me look upon the war in Pakistan and to share the immense suffering that the world seems to be experiencing at this time. And Jesus is in the suffering. The resurrection is something we have very little way of comprehending, although I believe that the glimmers of his resurrection are being experienced in many ways. And so it seems to me that we have to be willing to sacrifice in order to attain peace.

Right now I am out here in the woods with my wife and children and we are thinking much about Jesus. We're sharing in him by daily prayer, by simple work on our farm, by meditating. We're not sure what the future holds for us but we are open to it because we feel that is what it means to be followers of Jesus.

How do you understand Jesus' message?

That we have to begin new life-styles—simple life-styles. We must begin to live what the Kingdom is about. We have to begin to divest ourselves of the things that most men and women need. We have to start giving away what we don't need, sharing with the poor, helping the wretched of the earth. And I don't mean that in an abstract way. I mean beginning in your neighborhood, in your home, finding ways of sharing our experience of Christ together in community, in families of Christians.

This is a great age, despite the immense suffering and the immense death that surround us. I think the joy of being a Christian in this age is that we can scratch hope on these walls of the cave of death that surround us. We can say, "Celebrate life in the name of God! Jesus Christ did come and he is here and he will come again."

What do you think of the current Jesus movement?

Young people are starving for spiritual food and we haven't been giving it to them. We don't know yet what historical meaning it is going to have because not enough time has passed. Still the Jesus movement holds great interest for me. But there are many movements, I think. The Spirit is moving in many areas, even in the ruins of the Catholic Church.

There is a real freedom happening now. You and I as Christians are beginning to see the possibilities of the invitation that Christ gave to those first apostles—an incredible invitation to become free men and women in his name, to become like him, to become like his Father.

Ethel Gintoft

Ethel Gintoft is the associate editor of the Catholic Herald Citizen, *the Milwaukee diocesan newspaper. She is the first lay woman on the Board of the Catholic Press Association.*

Why do you believe in Jesus?

I believe in Jesus because of the example of other

people. It was through the people around me at a Cursillo that he became real to me as a person. I saw unselfish people that I had not known before doing palanca (prayers and sacrifices) for me out of love for Christ and Christ's love for other people. I heard them talk about Christ and I saw people really living out his message. These people motivated me to study more about him and want to imitate him and find him in other people.

How would you describe your image of Jesus?

I think of him more in his humanness. I think of Jesus as someone so human that he probably didn't even realize his own divinity, at least in his earlier years. If he fully realized he was God, then somehow the agony in the garden wouldn't come off as real as it should. His crying out to God wouldn't be as real for me. He would be akin to a white man going into a black ghetto and saying, "I identify with the black completely." But he

couldn't possibly because, in fact, he isn't black, and he knows that when he wants he can get out.

How does Jesus affect your daily life?

He makes it pretty darn tough sometimes. He unsettles me and makes me feel tension and makes me realize how I really don't live up to his example. But at the same time I can take comfort in that unsettling insecurity and sense of failure because even the people he picked to follow him didn't *always* live up to what they thought they should do. Yet he still loved them. He just asked them to gradually grow and love him, and that is what he is doing in my life. On a day-to-day level he has helped me feel hope, for he did promise paradise and confirm it with his resurrection.

What does his resurrection mean to you?

I'm not theologically certain about what resurrection means (and I'll leave that to the theologians). But it means, at least minimally, that his Spirit is always among us and helps us to keep reaching for and evolving toward the perfection which he represents. I feel a surging hope that together in him we are going someplace.

What are your feelings about the present-day emphasis on Jesus in the pop culture?

I am glad that people are rediscovering Jesus. I am afraid, though, of some attitudes that say, "Oh, I accept Jesus now. Everything's O.K." I hope it goes on to a real imitation of him: his love of friend and enemy; his service to the poorest; his pacifism.

David DuPlessis is a Pentecostal minister who has spent 50 of his 66 years preaching about Jesus. A native of South Africa, Dr. DuPlessis says that his occupation is "being all things to all men."

Why do you believe in Jesus?

When I was a boy living with my parents on a mission station in South Africa, I saw how the Africans, who could neither read nor write, talked about Jesus as if they had met him, seen him, talked with him. I saw how he revolutionized their lives by bringing a kind of fellowship among them. And I knew it wasn't any catechism that had changed them; it was Jesus himself.

I had read through the Bible as a boy with my parents, but Jesus was not alive to me. He wasn't real until I saw how he affected the Africans. I saw the Bible as a history book. To them it was like receiving a letter today.

129

In 1916, I met Jesus as Savior. He changed my life in that I began to find that now I could love.

What effect does Jesus have on your daily life?

Jesus is my constant companion. I have developed the habit of talking to him. No matter what happens—whether in the plane, the train, at home—I just discuss everything with Jesus. And when I see things around that I don't like or things that grieve me, I discuss these with him and say, "Lord, can I do anything? What will you have me do about this?"

Jesus is so very real. I can hear him inside me. There are some things that become very real to me when I pray. I am aware that he is talking to me and guiding me. My whole life is wrapped up in Christ.

If Jesus came back to the world today, I believe he would change society by saying one thing: "Love one another." Love can happen when men learn forgiveness. And we can only learn to forgive each other with the help of God.

How do you picture Jesus?

I believe we make a big mistake if we portray Jesus Christ too narrowly. To the sick he was a healer. To the hungry he was the feeder. Christ came to men and presented his message in different forms. He is the answer to everyone's needs; it just depends on what you need.

I don't see any particular danger in allowing people to view Christ as they wish. I think the danger lies in the fact that we try to limit Christ.

About the Authors

Karen Katafiasz DiDomenico was formerly assistant editor of *St. Anthony Messenger*. A graduate of Marquette University College of Journalism, she now lives in Toledo, Ohio, and does free-lance writing.

Karen Wullenweber Hurley is an assistant editor of *St. Anthony Messenger*. She holds a B.A. in philosophy from Edgecliff College, Cincinnati, and a M.A. in theology from the University of Notre Dame.

Father Leonard Foley, O.F.M., book editor of St. Anthony Messenger Press and editor of *Homily Helps* for priests, has had varied experiences as teacher, parish priest, retreat master, and editor of *St. Anthony Messenger*. His latest book is entitled *Signs of Love: The Sacraments of Christ*.

Father Eugene H. Maly holds a doctorate in Sacred Scripture, which he teaches at Mt. St. Mary Seminary, Cincinnati. At Vatican II he served as an official theologian. He is a past president of the Biblical Association of America. He is the editorial chairman of *The Bible Today* and has authored many articles and books.

Kenneth Eberhard earned his master's in theology at the University of San Francisco and his doctorate at the Graduate Theological Union, Berkeley. He presently teaches theology at the University of Santa Clara. His book *The Alienated Christian* appeared in 1971 and he will soon publish a book on the meaning of being a Catholic today.